KACHINAS: a Hopi artist's documentary

KACHINAS:

Original paintings by Cliff Bahnimptewa

a Hopi artist's documentary

by BARTON WRIGHT
CURATOR OF THE MUSEUM OF NORTHERN ARIZONA

Foreword by Patrick T. Houlihan
DIRECTOR OF THE HEARD MUSEUM

Published by Northland Press, Flagstaff with the Heard Museum, Phoenix

The Nichols' collection of paintings by Cliff Bahnimptewa is presently on extended loan to The Heard Museum for the purposes of exhibition, education and study.

ISBN 0-87358-110-5

Library of Congress Catalog Card Number 73-75204

Composed and Printed in the United States of America

To Dean Nichols

Contents

Foreword

As an introduction to Hopi Kachinas this book is twofold in purpose. First, it seeks to present 237 paintings of Kachinas by a single Hopi artist. Second, the accompanying text by Barton Wright is intended to place the Hopi Kachina in its cultural perspective. From this combination of artist and social scientist, participant and observer it is hoped that this one artifact of Hopi religion and art can be more thoughtfully and accurately known.

The book is intended to reach both scholar and layman. For both it presents a glimpse at the knowledge of Hopi culture Barton Wright has gained from nearly twenty years work with the Hopi; and by the juxtaposition of text and painting is sought a "flash card" identification of Hopi Kachinas. The need for more accurate information and illustration of Hopi Kachinas has been made especially acute with the growth of interest in Native American Art and in Kachinas as one expression of that art. And since a great many of the Kachinas depicted may be rare or no longer current, this publication of the Cliff Bahnimptewa series is a valuable contribution to the knowledge of Kachinas. This, and the fact that Native Americans very rarely "tell their own story," heightens the import of this work.

The history of *Kachinas: A Hopi Artist's Documentary* begins in north central Arizona where Mr. Don Hoel of Oak Creek Canyon suggested to Dr. and Mrs. Dean Nichols of Phoenix that a single Hopi artist's perception of Kachinas be recorded. With the Nichols' support, Cliff Bahnimptewa, a Hopi Kachina carver from Third Mesa was commissioned to paint a series of Kachinas. Dr. Harold Colton's *Hopi Kachina Dolls with a Key to their Identification* served as a check list, and most of the Kachina paintings presented here are also listed in Colton. Although the Colton list has been used as a basis, the Bahnimptewa series records one man's understanding of the conventions of an essential part of Hopi religion, the costuming and appearance of the rain-bringing guardian spirits.

The Bahnimptewa paintings were first shown to the public in 1971 at The Heard Museum Gallery of Indian Art. In conjunction with this exhibition, a catalogue entitled *Dancing Kachinas* was published and forty-eight smaller photographs of the paintings were reproduced there. The response to this exhibit and catalogue then prompted The Heard Museum to consider this larger publication. Barton Wright was the unanimous choice to author the accompanying text and he, along with H. Thomas Cain, Richard Conn, Dr. Bertha P. Dutton, Dr. Edward B. Danson, Byron Harvey and Paul Weaver, contributed immeasurably at the initial planning stages of the volume.

It is the hope of The Heard Museum that this volume is but the first of a series of major publications devoted to the Native American and his Art.

PATRICK T. HOULIHAN

Acknowledgments

SUPPORT FOR THIS PUBLICATION has been as generous as it has been diverse. The principal encouragement for this book has come from Dr. and Mrs. Dean Nichols. The Nichols along with Mrs. John W. Kieckhefer, Mrs. John C. Lincoln, and Mrs. Wallace Thorne monetarily helped to make this book a reality.

Mr. Edward Jacobson, Mr. Edward F. Lowry, Jr., Mrs. John O'Connor, Mr. James V. Parker, and Miss Evelyn Roat contributed greatly of their time and professional expertise.

And finally, as a body, the Trustees of The Heard Museum are acknowledged for their support of this volume.

Introduction

WITHIN THE SOUTHWESTERN QUADRANT of the United States lies an amorphous area called the Southwest. Its geographical limits are rather difficult to define since it includes all of Arizona and New Mexico and portions of the adjacent states of Utah and Colorado, in addition to parts of northwestern Mexico. It has been described by anthropologists as a "culture area" and the Indian tribes within it have been treated individually and as an interrelated whole.

The land of the Southwest is one of searing desert and towering peaks, but between these extremes are areas suitable for human occupation. The majority of Southwestern Indian tribes are to be found in the uplands, on the flanks of the high mountains among piñon pines and juniper. Here access is easy to both the game of the highlands and to the protein-rich seeds of the desert plants.

These Southwestern tribes represent two modes of adaptation: the sedentary people occupying small villages and raising crops; and the nomadic groups that depended on hunting and more recently on the raising of livestock. Often the two occupy the same land, though using it for different purposes. It is the sedentary Indians of Arizona and New Mexico, those dwelling in small communities of tightly packed houses that the Spanish Conquistadores called "pueblos," with whom we are concerned in this book.

Farmers in any part of the world have always been dependent on the weather for successful crops, and the Pueblo people have been contending with the vagaries of the Southwest's weather patterns for more than 2000 years. In the course of that time they have accumulated a store of commonsense observations on what may happen if certain conditions prevail, and with this knowledge has come a relatively accurate system of weather prediction.

However, this is really not enough to survive the erratic weather conditions of their semiarid land. Hence the Pueblo peoples evolved an elaborate pattern for securing help from the supernatural forces that are believed to control nature. All of the Pueblos have this complex religious pattern, though in some groups it is more elaborate than in others.

The Hopi Indians are the westernmost of the Pueblo peoples and live in twelve villages set on the three mesas in northeastern Arizona. These are called First Mesa, Second Mesa and Third Mesa in order of their access from the east. To grow crops, particularly corn, in their semiarid land the Hopis believe it is absolutely essential to have the supernaturals on their side. However, the Hopis do not approach their supernaturals as we do. The Hopis feel that their supernaturals have certain powers which they do not have, and that they in turn possess things which their supernaturals desire. Thus quite often Hopi rituals are mutual gift-giving ceremonies. The supernaturals desire prayer feathers, corn pollen and various rituals, and the Hopis like rain, so this mutual exchange works out very well for both parties.

While the Hopis' greatest ritual effort is devoted to securing favorable weather for good harvests, this is by no means all of the Hopi religion, a subject so extremely complex that volumes have been written about it. However, one aspect of it, important for this publication, is the Kachina cult. Within Hopi religion the Kachina cult has probably been elaborated on more than those among any of the neighboring pueblos.

The Kachina cult has been described as a common denominator in Hopi religion. Nearly every Hopi takes part in it, and Kachinas are a popular and much discussed feature of Hopi life. Hopi Kachinas are supernaturals, embodying the spirits of living things and also the spirits of ancestors who have died and become a part of nature. Kachinas are believed to possess powers over nature, especially the weather, but higher gods limit the extent of their powers.

There are still other supernaturals in the Hopi pantheon that are not Kachinas, but which affect Kachinas.

To Hopis, it is essential to preserve harmony with the world around them, not only with man and other animals but with objects in nature such as rocks, clouds, sky, etc., which the Hopis believe to be possessed of life. Since the Kachinas embody these spirits they are the spiritual guardians of the Hopi people and their way of life. And since they can insure human, animal and plant fertility, they insure life itself. Hopi men carve likenesses of the Kachinas from cottonwood root, and these are the well-known Kachina dolls that are of special interest to collectors.

In the yearly cycle of religious ceremonies, Kachina dances are preeminent. However, the term "dance" does not have the same meaning as the Western notion of social or interpretive dance. In Hopi dances, the Kachinas are personated by Hopi men, age ten to eighty, and these dances constitute the subjects of Clifford Bah-nimptewa's paintings here.

When Kachinas are personated by the men of the villages, they assume visual form and appear in the streets and plazas of the town. It is here that the Kachina is his most magnificent, for the Hopis feel that when they impersonate a Kachina they *become* the supernatural. As supernaturals they may cure disease, grow corn, bring clouds and rain, watch over ceremonies and reinforce discipline and order in the Hopi world.

Because there are many circumstances that arise requiring supernatural help, there are many Kachinas. Among the Hopi there are about 300 Kachinas that may be current, and at least another 200 that may be known but make only sporadic appearances. It is perfectly consistent that Kachinas may wane and new ones appear as the needs of the Hopis change. Thus some Kachinas remain only in appearance, with all thought of their original purpose lost, or some will fade from memory entirely. At the other extreme will be Kachinas that are not more than a few years old.

Each Kachina has a particular marking or symbol that identifies it to the watching Hopi. Less apparent are details of costume that are essential to the different types of Kachinas. There are many Kachinas that represent elements in the world of the Hopi, such as plants, animals, clouds, abstract forms, stars and sky. Everything that surrounds the Hopi may have a supernatural associated with it, and it is thus possible to have an Ashes Kachina or a Jimson Weed Kachina. In addition there are Kachinas that represent the spirit of the Hopi's neighbors, the Navajo or the Zuñi, the Havasupai or the Apache. These may be caricatures or earnest representations.

One group of Kachinas, the Chief Kachinas, correspond to the village leaders and are most important. They have jurisdiction over other Kachinas and the more important aspects of village life. These Kachinas, which are rather few in number, are never changed and appear at every important ceremony with which they are connected. They are treated with great respect, and usually dolls or other representations are not made of them. If they are made, it is essential that their representation be as accurate as possible.

There is another group of Kachinas that might be described as warriors or guards or police. They oversee the handling of particular events, making sure that the audience does not approach the wrong area or interfere with the dancers. Some of them serve to enforce community projects, insuring that Hopi men attend and perform their duties. Others bear war symbolism which refers back in time to the period when the Hopis were under attack by hostile neighbors. Although the Hopis are considered peaceful, the necessity for defense in the past is commemorated in the spears carried by certain Kachinas, in the designs symbolizing bravery, and in particular Kachinas such as the Warrior Maid who saved her village when it was under attack.

The Kachina calendar begins with the appearance of the important Kachinas in January. At this time Chief Kachinas bless certain portions of the village and perform rituals designed to open the season for other Kachina performances. The second major ceremony — *Powamu* — occurs in February and is accompanied by the magical appearance of green growing plants while the land is still locked in the grip of winter. At *Powamu* or "Bean Dance" large numbers of Kachinas appear but usually do not dance. At times when the young men of the village are initiated into the tribe (not to be confused with the annual initiation of the children into the Kachina cult), the *Powamu* ceremony may be even larger, and rarer Kachinas make their appearance. In March, the Night Dances are held in the kivas, for it is still too cold to dance in the plaza. These dances are generally similar to the Plaza Dances which are held later in the spring. Plaza Dances are composed of line dancers, with many performers representing a single Kachina or a mixed group of similar figures. The greater amount of space in the plaza provides room for the long lines of regular dancers and for the more active "side dancers." These highly skilled "side dancers" encourage the others and emphasize the rhythm of the song and often accompany the words of the songs with gestures. Summer Dances are always popular and well attended. The final dance of the year is the "Home Dance" or *Niman*. It signals the departure of all the Kachinas for their mountain homes. After the "Home Dance" no more Kachinas appear until the following year.

The Kachinas, then, occupy much of the ceremonial year. They distribute food and blessings, accept prayers, provide entertainment, and reflect many features of Hopi life. In addition, there are many important family relationships among the Kachinas. The women (*Kachin-mana*) are sisters or wives of the male dancers. Kachinas may have aunts, uncles, or grandfathers so that life among the supernaturals seems to emphasize the order of a Hopi family. In the Kachina dances, the Kachina women (normally impersonated by men), grind corn in a ritual enactment by the use of rasps and gourd resonators, and this is accompanied by the Kachina men's distribution of food. In this giving, the farmers' produce is shared by the entire community. During the day, the villagers often feast in various relatives' homes, enjoying themselves and reinforcing their ties of family and clan kinship.

Thus, entertainment, discipline, teaching, explanations of nature and reflections of the Hopi past all blend together in the Kachina cult. In fact, the many different aspects of Kachinas and their flexibility help explain their importance and popularity. The large number of figures insures enough variety that one or another may be revived or emphasized or seemingly forgotten for years.

As each of the twelve Hopi villages progresses at its own rate of development entirely separate from its neighbors, it is possible for one village to retain a similar name for a widely variant Kachina, or for a Kachina to be lost completely in one village and still be seen in another. Consequently, when Kachinas are represented in paintings or carvings, it is essential to know from which village the individual making the representation comes and what his age is. For with age comes a better understanding of Kachinas. Thus, for example, a ten-year-old Hopi boy has only a superficial knowledge of the Kachina that he dances. As he moves through initiation into the tribe and becomes a man he gains more and more knowledge until he may assume a chief's status within the village. It is impossible for a Hopi to take a short cut in this temporal advancement. Hence, a young man cannot know all of the attributes of Kachinas. It is not because of a lack of interest or observation but because of his youth. To evaluate the creator's knowledge of Kachinas in representations such as these paintings, one must be aware of the geographical location, temporal location and age of the interpreter.

Clifford Bahnimptewa is a young man from the village of Old Oraibi on Third Mesa, hence his knowledge of Kachinas is that of a young man. And while he is not a professional artist his paintings are realistic renderings of single dancers in which each figure appears as if in a performance. His full figure renditions convey with immediacy and effectiveness the Hopi Kachina Dancers.

BARTON WRIGHT

THE KACHINAS

SOLSTICE KACHINAS

EACH YEAR the opening ceremony of the Kachina Season is performed by the Solstice or "Return" Kachinas. Their appearance, after a six-month absence, signals the starting of a new Hopi year for no other kachina may be seen on the mesas until this ritual is completed. These kachinas appear after the Wuwuchim Ceremony, which is held in late November, and at a precise interval before the Winter Solstice. Only Third Mesa has a single figure, the Soyal Kachina, to announce the approaching Solstice ceremony to start the new Kachina Season.

If one were standing in Oraibi (on Third Mesa) early in December he might see a solitary figure making its feeble and uncertain way in the late afternoon sun from the southern mesa edge to the village. Dressed in shabby, worn clothes, and tottering along with the stumbling movements of an old man, the first kachina of the year enters the village, often almost unnoticed by its inhabitants. Following a set path the Solstice or Soyal Kachina proceeds, singing a song too sacred or too low to be heard by bystanders; creakily performing a dance, he stops at a certain kiva and places prayer feathers and sprinkles cornmeal. When he has visited the kiva and the plaza and completed his ritual he makes his uncertain way out of the village and disappears having opened the kachina season for the coming year.

Soyal

This Third Mesa Soyal holds in his left hand the standard or symbol of the Soyal Ceremony: four long switches with feathers at intervals along their length. Normally the feathers that appear on the sticks are flicker feathers, but here they are represented as eagle breast feathers. The artist has made an attempt to catch the old and worn appearance of the hunting shirt that the kachina wears.

SOYAL CEREMONY

THE SOYAL is the winter solstice ceremony and with its beginning other kachinas make their appearance. For some mesas and villages this will be the first appearance of any kachina. The primary ritual is conceived as helping to turn the sun back toward its summer path. Woven around this concept are many others that involve the entire community in one respect or another. On Second and Third Mesas there is a war ritual in which medicine is prepared that all members of the village may either drink or smear on themselves for health and strength. On First Mesa this occurs after the Soyal, but there is an appearance of a masked War Chief that does not occur on Second and Third Mesas. Corn of all colors that is ritually tied with yucca fiber is brought into the kivas for consecration. On Third Mesa the consecrated corn is returned to the women by four unmasked individuals while on First Mesa it is symbolically paraded by Ahülani and the two Corn Maidens before being returned.

Pahos (prayer feathers) are prepared by groups and individuals for every conceivable purpose. Prayer feathers are prepared for relatives, family and friends; for the increase of animals and crops; for houses and cars; and for personal well being; and prayer objects are made by the kiva group for the village. On Third Mesa the Mastop Kachinas appear and symbolically fertilize all the females of the village. A different kachina but one with a similar purpose appears on Second Mesa during initiation years. There is no known kachina that is comparable on First Mesa. The final day of the Soyal on Third Mesa is characterized by the appearance of the Qöqöqolom and their Kachin Manas who appear and "open the kivas" by marking the hatchways with cornmeal. On First Mesa it is Ahülani and the Corn Maidens who open the kivas with their appearance in the village, while on Second Mesa, it is Ahül and a single mana that perform this function.

8

Ahöla

Ahöla is an important chief kachina for both First and Second Mesa as he opens the Powamu ceremony with a kiva performance on the first night. This performance seems to involve mimetic magic to slow the passage of the sun. At a shrine in the "Gap" of First Mesa the next day an additional rite is performed as the sun rises. With daybreak Ahul (or Ahöla) and the Powamu Chief deposit pahos (prayer feathers) at Kachina Spring, for he is the ancient one of the Kachina Clan. As the ancient one he led the people from the San Francisco Peaks eastward as far as the great river and then westward to where they were stopped by the turbulent waters and where their houses still stand. After going to the Kachina Spring, Ahöla and the Powamu Chief then visit all of the kivas and houses with ceremonial associations, distributing the Powamu Chief's bean and corn plants and marking the entrances with four stripes of meal, thereby appealing to the Cloud Chiefs to sit over these places. At the end of this ceremony Ahöla descends to a shrine where he bows four times to the Sun and asks for long life, health, happiness and good crops for his children.

Ahöl Mana

Ahöl Mana occurs only on Second Mesa at the time of the Soyal. She is a standard Kachin Mana except that she comes with Ahöla which by context makes her Ahöl Mana. She accompanies Ahöla on his rounds to the various kivas and ceremonial houses. In her hands she holds a tray with various kinds of seeds from the fields of the Kachina Chief. The artist has put the Kachin Mana in an embroidered wedding robe which she does not wear on Second Mesa and has put bean sprouts in the tray thus making her resemble a Pachava Mana.

Kaletaka

This version of Kaletaka is the first one mentioned in this kachina category by Colton (1959:21:#4). The second variety is Akush and not Kaletaka. The First Mesa Kaletaka makes a single appearance in this form during the Soyal. He accompanies Ahülani from a shrine east of the village to the kiva where Ahülani later makes his appearance. Kaletaka carries a bow in his left hand and arrows in his right hand. His body is all black with white smears as shown, and the same should be true of the legs rather than the long knit stockings shown. The bandoliers that are worn are stained red and twisted. The ears have eagle feathers inserted through them.

Qöqöle

Third Mesa is the only place where the Qöqöle appears during the Soyal. He comes in a large group of many Qöqöle and their manas, on the last day of the ceremony. Combining ritual with pleasure they burlesque other ceremonies while at the same time managing to "open" the kivas. Thus it is possible that at one moment the kachina may be very seriously marking the four sides of the kivas to allow the other kachinas to come and visit the village, and at the next moment be kneeling on the ground to shoot marbles. Frequently they imitate the women's dances of the preceding fall. Third Mesa Qöqöle has one other aspect that sets him apart from almost all other kachinas. He wears old Anglo clothing. Formerly he may have appeared in the buckskins that are seen on Second Mesa, but at present he does not appear this way on Third Mesa. More often than not the kachina appears with a black face and blue markings, although he can theoretically appear in any color because he is a directional kachina. As each direction has a color he could appear in a color combination representing any of the six directions. This is a very good painting of a Third Mesa Qöqöle who is kneeling to play marbles during one of the antic moments of his appearance.

Mastop

The Mastop Kachina is the second kachina to appear on Third Mesa. He is not present on Second or First Mesa. These kachinas always arrive in pairs and come bounding out of the northwest on the next to last day of the Soyal. As they rush into the village they beat all the dogs that they encounter using the short black and white staff which they carry for that purpose. Leaping about with many antic gestures, they make their way to the Chief Kiva where they talk in disguised voices with the individuals inside and with each other. Then, as though suddenly becoming aware of the females in the audience, they dash madly into a cluster of women and grab their shoulders from behind and they give a series of small hops indicating copulation. Then they return to the kiva and converse for a while before again dashing over to another group of women, repeating the action until nearly every woman present from child to the very oldest has been approached. All women, even the shy ones, do not avoid this embrace as it is a serious fertility rite despite the antic touches, which are never directed towards the women.

Ahülani

Ahülani makes his quiet appearance rather late in the afternoon of the sixth day of the Soyal Ceremony when he rises rather creakily from one of the kivas with his two maidens. He and his two maids function almost exactly as does the Soyal Kachina of Third Mesa in that no other kachina may appear before them. In essence he is the announcer of the coming kachina season just as is Soyal. However, Ahülani, Kachin Mana (Yellow Corn Girl, and Sakwap Mana (Blue Corn Girl) appear during the Soyal rather than sixteen days before. Together the trio arrange themselves near the kiva hatchway and face east. Ahülani plants his staff firmly on the ground and they begin to sing. As each chorus is finished they pace slowly forward a step for each part of the song until it is completed. Making his dignified way to the plaza, followed by the two manas with their burdens of corn, he repeats the same ritual there and in other parts of the village before they return to the kiva and disappear. This ceremonial circuit of the village, bearing token corn, is the last act before the seed corn that has been consecrated in the kiva is returned to the owners. Ahülani appears in two very distinct forms; one variety is seen only on the years when the Snake Dance is held on First Mesa and the other when the Flute Dance is held on that mesa. The artist has here shown Ahülani as he would appear during the year that the Flute Dance is held. The artist has failed to show the cape that normally covers him from the shoulders to slightly below the waist. As he is accompanied by maidens bearing seed corn in trays, Ahülani does not carry a tray in this performance. Rather he holds a staff in his right hand and chieftain gear in his left hand.

Sakwap Mana

Sakwap Mana is so called because she carries a tray of blue corn; otherwise she is a standard Kachin Mana. The corn that she carries is stacked in a ring on a flat tray with the ears set on end, and these are surrounded by spruce boughs. The artist has chosen to portray the version of Kachin Mana that is called Takurs Mana but he has also given her the tray of blue corn that is necessary for her to be called Sakwap Mana and this is incorrect.

Kachin Mana

Kachin Mana in this context is called Yellow Corn Girl and carries a tray of corn exactly the same as Sakwap Mana except that it is yellow. This illustration is a good one of the Kachin Mana but does not show her as she would appear as the Yellow Corn Girl.

16

THE POWAMU is one of the most important of the Hopi ceremonies. It occurs in February of each year in most of the Hopi villages. In actuality it is not a single ceremony but a cluster of several important events that are interwoven. Most years the ceremony is presented in an abbreviated form. However, in the years when the tribal initiation of the young men is held, the Pachavu Ceremony will be attached to the Powamu, and the ceremony is presented in its full, unabridged form.

Undoubtedly the most important aspect of the Powamu ceremony is the anticipation of the coming growing season, with ritual designed to promote fertility and germination. To accomplish this the Powamu chief appears as Muyingwa, the principal deity of germination, and every male who has been initiated into the Kachina cult is expected to grow beans in the kivas. The growing of these bean sprouts gives the ceremony its popular name, and offers omens for the success of the coming growing season. The ceremonial procession of the Pachavu Manas carrying these bean sprouts and the presentation of ritual bundles of them to the women and children during the height of the winter are tangible evidence of the presence of Muyingwa.

Second in importance is the initiation of the children into the Kachina Society at this time. Powamu officers serve as fathers of the kachinas at this time reinforcing the relationship between the Powamu and Kachina cult.

Incorporated into the Powamu are historical or mythological events which are given as dramatic presentations. The relationships between the Village Chief and his clan with the clans of other chiefs are emphasized. Most of these events are accompanied by the impersonation of a great many Chief Kachinas. These presentations allow all men and kachinas in positions of authority to appear with their badges of authority before the village.

In addition to these rites there is a strong educational aspect that appears throughout the entire ceremony. The incorporation of the Soyoko ceremony with its disciplinary emphasis on the younger children and the feeling that all have bought their lives for another year is a part of this. The whipping of the children who are initiated to emphasize the need for secrecy might also be included.

The presentation of these rituals brings forth an enormous number of kachinas. Some of these are present year after year while others may be present but never be seen by outsiders or, for that matter, by most of the Hopis. Other kachinas appear only during Pachavu or Initiation or at irregular intervals.

Eototo

One of the kachinas that appears each year is Eototo.
On each of the three mesas he is the spiritual counterpart of
the Village Chief and as such is called the "father"
of the kachinas. He is the chief of all kachinas and knows
every ceremony. As father or chief of the kachinas he
appears in all major ceremonies. At Third Mesa during
the Powamu, Eototo and Aholi come out of the Chief
Kiva. Eototo always leads, and he draws cornmeal
symbols of clouds on the ground. Aholi places his
staff on the symbol and waves it in an all-encompassing
fashion while giving a long call. This performance
is the blessing of the village and marking it so that the
clouds will come to the pueblo. A ceremonially prepared
hole in the plaza is marked with cornmeal lines leading to
it for the clouds to follow, and then water is poured
into the hole which represents the town cisterns. The
water is from Eototo's gourd of sacred water (mimetic
magic to induce a desired occurrence). Arriving at
the Powamu Kiva where the Crow Mother awaits, Eototo
again draws lines leading to the hatchway from the
different directions and then pours water from his gourd
into the hatchway where it is caught in a basin by the
Powamu Kiva Chief below. At each blessing Eototo is
given prayer feathers and the kiva chief takes some of the
corn sprouts that he carries under his arm. Aholi
faithfully repeats each action. Again these actions are to
bring water to the village and its growing crops, symbolized
by the bean sprouts in the kiva. The role that Eototo
plays in each ceremony is complex and is only most
briefly summarized here. This illustration is that of a
Third Mesa Eototo.

Aholi

Aholi appears only on Third Mesa and in the company of Eototo during the Powamu Ceremony. This kachina is the ancient of the Pikyas Clan. Legend has it that Aholi, left behind to fight a rear guard action, later followed Eototo through migrations that took them from Mexico to Utah and from the Colorado River to the Rio Grande and back to their present location on Third Mesa. The two kachinas come out of the Chief Kiva during Powamu and perform the rites described under Eototo. Aholi is a beautiful kachina in his multi-colored cloak and tall blue helmet, but he is of less importance than the very plain Eototo and is often called Eototo's Lieutenant. When Eototo places his cloud mark on the ground, Aholi puts the butt of his staff upon it and swinging the staff around calls out, "Ah-holi--i-i-i," and then follows his chief to the next mark. His actions appear to be a reinforcing of Eototo's actions. This illustration portrays the kachina as he leans forward to place the butt of his staff upon Eototo's mark.

Kokosori

This small kachina, for he is always portrayed by a boy, is one of the oldest recorded kachinas for the Hopis, as Dr. Ten Broeck saw him in 1852 at First Mesa. He appears in other pueblos but is probably best known in Zuni where his name is Shulawitsi. It is this tie with Zuni that brings his appearance on First Mesa with other Zuni Kachinas in the Pamuiti Ceremony described by Fewkes (1903:27). He has on occasion appeared as a Barter Kachina also on First Mesa. On Second Mesa he bears the name of Kokoshoya and comes with the Chief Kachinas in their appearance after the story-telling of the Sikyaqöqöqolom (the Yellow Qöqöle) at Powamu. On Third Mesa the small figure of Kokosori is said to accompany Aholi and Eototo. The artist has portrayed him as he might appear in Anktioni performances (the Night Dances that follow the Powamu) at Third Mesa. However he has placed many items in his hands that are usually assigned to specific ceremonies rather than appearing all at once.

A-ha

A-ha is one of the Chief Kachinas of Second
Mesa and appears only on this mesa during the Powamu
or Bean Dance. He is known by either of two names,
A-ha or Kuzrua. He appears in a short kiva rite
after the performance of the Sikyaqöqöqolom with Ahöla,
Eototo and Kokoshoya when they bring their blessings
to the village and again during the very important
Pachavu Ceremony. This is drawn as described in Colton
with the exception of the eyes which are rectangular —
the right one is blue and the left one is yellow.

A-ha Kachin Mana

The maiden who appears with A-ha is another representation of the Kachin Mana (HSC-133). She differs in no major respect from the Kachin Mana, carries no special things in her hands and cannot be distinguished as A-ha Mana except by her association with A-ha.

Angwushahai-i

Angwushahai-i is the Crow Mother, Angwusnasomtaka, in a different guise. On Third Mesa it is said that Angwushahai-i is the one who initiates the children and talks to the whippers, and it is Angwusnasomtaka that appears dressed all in white on the last day of Powamu. Still others from Third Mesa say that the figure in white is that of Angwushahai-i. As the Crow Bride she performs a role quite apart from her appearance as the Crow Mother. There is a legend that relates her journey as a bride and her return as a married woman. As the Crow Bride she appears at second dawning to the east of the village and moves slowly toward the town bearing in her hands a large tray of corn sprouts. Entering the village she pauses and begins to sing in a subdued voice. Completing the song she moves sedately forward to another point and again pauses to repeat the performance. At each pause women come forward to take one of the corn sprouts from her tray and to cast meal upon her. Her slow progress eventually brings her at full dawn to the Chief Kiva where the kiva chiefs await her and where at Oraibi she is joined by Eototo and Aholi. Here the Kachinas are given prayer feathers and meal and then dismissed. The Crow Bride then makes her dignified way out of the village to the southwest and disappears toward her home, the San Francisco Peaks.

Tungwup Ta-amu

Despite the fact that this figure is known as the Whipper's Uncle, he does not appear with the Hu or Tungwup Kachinas who initiate the children. Instead he appears as a guard during the Bean Dance Parade or Procession on Second and Third Mesa. Fewkes lists him as belonging to the Tungwup group on First Mesa but does not at any time place him in the initiation group in his descriptions. Thus it would seem that he is the uncle of other whipper kachinas and should possibly appear in the Mixed Dances. Discounting many small variations, this kachina is quite similar to the one who appeared on First Mesa at the turn of the century.

Qöchaf Kachina

Qöchaf Kachina is one who occurs only on Second Mesa at the villages of Shungopovi and Shipaulovi. Just as ashes are used to purify objects during various ceremonies, the Ashes Kachina (Qöchaf) is used to purify the village, everyone and all things. He appears on the last day of Powamu and his arrival signals the beginning of the Bean Dance Procession. The artist's portrayal does not approximate the actual kachina. The mouth of the kachina is square and in this illustration the artist inadvertently omitted painting it. In reality the lower arms are blackened, the kilt of the old dress is adorned with cornhusk stars and a fox fur hangs to the rear. Around his ankles he usually wears embroidered anklets.

Wuyak-kuita

In every ceremony there are guards to prevent
any transgression on the path of the kachinas. In addition,
guards or Angry Kachinas were formerly used to enforce
community work such as the cleaning of springs. It
is to this category that the Wuyak-kuita belongs. There
is evidence that this kachina has many forms that
have changed through time. Wuyak-kuita is most often
seen bringing up the rear of the Bean Dance Procession
or circling wide at the sides. He is the one who moves
toward the clowns and absolutely terrifies them. On
Third Mesa these are the kachinas who guard the kivas to
keep Hé-é-e from approaching too close during the
Palölökong Ceremony, or from going to the Flute Spring
during the same ceremony. This form of the kachina is the
one most commonly seen at ceremonies like the Powamu.

Chaveyo

Chaveyo is one of the more cosmopolitan kachinas. He is represented in nearly every pueblo, but his original home was probably in the San Juan area of New Mexico. However, for the Hopis his home is the San Francisco Mountains, and he is the husband of Hahai-i Wuhti. The family of Hahai-i Wuhti and Chaveyo are the Nataskas, the dreadful Sosoyok't. Chaveyo is the Sergeant Snorkle of the kachinas. Should any Hopi fail to meet his obligations in community work or transgress the unspoken rules of conduct for the village, Chaveyo will show him the error of his ways. Chaveyo often appears with Soyoko on First Mesa but can appear for the same purpose anytime during the spring months. However, he is usually seen in the Powamu or Palölökongti (Water Serpent Dance) being badgered by the clowns who eventually will be soundly whacked for their efforts. This "giant" kachina is a favorite of kachina carvers and his irritable cantankerousness usually shows in the dolls that represent him. Those who see him for the first time at a kachina dance usually remember the kachina with "all those feathers and a sword." Interestingly enough the artist has drawn a mixture of the kachina as he appears on all three mesas. The stance is the most characteristic as he lifts the hair out of his eyes so that he may see who is bedeviling him.

Hó-e

As the procession of the Bean Dance proceeds around the village there are usually two or three of these clowns in the vanguard somewhere. They are noisy, boisterous teases. One minute they will have organized a Plains Contest Dance that knocks the other kachinas about while the next moment they will have a foot race underway that will go right through the middle of a group of kachinas. They will tease the guards or lure the Kwikwilyaka into mocking one of the Angry Kachinas. Wherever they are, the uproar is continuous, and they are the last to give up and go into the kiva. Time and again the Guardian Kachinas must return to a plaza to make sure the Hó-e keep up with the procession as they get carried away with their fun. It is possible to follow their progress by watching the heads of the Hopi youngsters which point to them like a compass to the north pole. The illustration shows one of the Hó-e holding up a doll of himself that he is going to give to one of the children in the audience, but he has not yet found the individual that he wants to present it to.

28

Wupamo

Wupamo appears on all three mesas as a guard, and the whips that he carries are for use on the unwary. Usually he may be found during the Powamu procession circling out from the sides or swinging in at the rear to spur the laggards. He moves a little more quickly than Wuyak-kuita but just as surely. On First Mesa as one of the Furious Kachinas he is often led or rather held back by a rope around his waist that is held by a Koyemsi. He is given to making short furious dashes towards the audience or other kachinas or kiva priests much in the manner of an erratic dog. In addition to the Powamu he may appear in the Palölökong or help enforce community work such as spring cleaning. It is strange that this illustration, which is correct in almost all details, should fail to convey the impression of this very important kachina. Ordinarily the nose bends very slightly down along its length, and there are teeth that show along the length of the snout. Here the head appears naked, and it does not when the actual kachina is seen.

Tsitoto

Tsitoto is an ancient kachina who appears on
all three mesas in many ceremonies. He may appear in the
Palölökong Ceremony and the Mixed Kachina Dances
as well as in the Powamu and Pachavu Ceremonies.
The many bands of color and the multicolored feathers
present a rainbow-like appearance, and he looks like a
walking prayer for summer. However, at least one of
his functions seems to be purification. In this role he
carries a small bunch of yucca blades and strikes each
individual that he meets a rather firm blow whether
he be a child or an adult, Hopi or White. The kachina
appears like this most often in the Bean Dance.

Tokoch Kachina

Tokotsi or Tokoch Kachina is the Wildcat Kachina. He is one of the Angry Kachinas and appears with others of this type when there is work to be done in the community such as the cleaning of the springs. He never appears in regular dances unless it is the Soyohim or Mixed Kachina Dance. As a kachina who is expected to keep the idlers at work, he usually carries a rope in his left hand and a switch in his right. There is a completely different Tokoch Kachina on Second Mesa (not shown here). He is usually represented with long hair streaming down over his eyes, and he is continually brushing it aside as he watches for any shirkers. This particular illustration has a poor representation of the wildcat skin over the back, and the painting of the body does not follow the usual pattern.

Left-handed Kachina

This fussy little kachina is called "Left-handed" because he carries his bow in his right hand instead of his left, and in fact most of his gear is reversed. Colton credits him with being derived from the Hualapai Indians but some Hopis say that he came from the Chemehuevi. He appears in a great many dances, like the Mixed Kachina, in groups in the kivas or separately as a warrior in the Powamu Ceremony. In addition, he is a favorite subject for the carving of kachina dolls or the painting of pictures. He may act as a prompter in a dance or be found making odd little bows and taking small mincing steps at the edge of a procession. A great deal of the time he has trouble with Hó-e when they appear in the same dance. Here one of the usual pair keeps up a steady step while the other points to evidence of a bear that they are obviously hunting.

Nuvak´china

The Snow Kachina is a favorite impersonation during the winter months. Because he lives on top of the San Francisco Peaks he is thought of as bringing the cold and snows to the Hopis. This winter moisture is absolutely essential for the growth of the crops. Hence Nuvak´ china appears in many winter ceremonies, the Soyal, Powamu, Palölökongti and the Mixed Dances of early spring. Since he is intimately associated with water, there is an alliance between him and the Water Serpent. Thus we find him dancing at a spring that belongs to the Water Serpent and must be cleaned out. Many times the Snow Kachina is used to distribute presents on the morning of the Bean Dance.

With this kachina's connotations it is inevitable that he would appear emblazoned on billboards advertising anything from ski runs to cold weather clothing. This Snow Kachina is the type that appears on Third Mesa.

Horo Mana

The name of this Tewa Kachina is given in
Colton's book as Horo Mana, but she is usually known by
the name of Yohozro Wuhti, the Cold-Bringing Woman.
Her most common appearance is on First Mesa during
the Powamu. She carries a Hopi comb in her hand to
muss up people's hair when she appears with Nuvak'
china, her grandson. This kachina appears all in white.
As her name implies, she brings the whiteness of winter.

Wukoqöte

The personation of Wukoqöte is split into several roles that are very difficult to unravel. However, the basic problem is that when he is spoken of on First Mesa he is in the form illustrated here. But when Second or Third Mesa Hopis speak of Wukoqöte he more closely resembles a Duck Kachina, and the functions vary accordingly. The First Mesa Wukoqöte is most often associated with the Powamu, Pachavu and Palölökong as a sergeant-at-arms. Usually they are seen in pairs roaming about the village, summoning delinquents to the kiva and making sure that the kiva members do not lie down at the wrong time. It is said that his appearance brings a gentle rain without thunder. The objects that Wukoqöte holds in his right hand are sheep scapulae, and a bow is held in his left hand.

35

Flute

The Flute or Lenang Kachina is most closely associated
in appearance and performance with the Powamu Kachina.
On First Mesa he makes his appearance during the
actual Bean Dance although, at times, he may be seen
during the Mixed Kachina Dances. Across his back is a
moisture tablet, in his hand is a flute whose mouthpiece
looks like a flower, and on his head are many replicas
of flowers done in wood. The Flute Kachina does not have
as many Zuni characteristics as it does Hopi despite its
many ties with Zuni. It is unfortunate that the artist
did not pick a pose for this kachina that would have shown
the flute and back tablet as well as the flowers on his head.

Kwikwilyaka

Kwikwilyaka is the Mocking Kachina. As a clown he has little personality of his own but fastens like a leech onto any activity that catches his eye. With mirror-like accuracy he will reflect every action of the unfortunate whom he decides to mimic. He drives the other kachinas such as Hó-e to strong measures to rid themselves of this unwanted echo. Should a person in the audience become the focus of this undesired attention, he must wait until something else diverts the kachina. But the wait is very difficult without inadvertently making some movement, and the rapidity of the mocking usually produces gales of laughter from the rest of the audience. During the Bean Dance procession he is a foil for the Hó-e and an annoyance to others.

Kwikwilyaka appears here in his ragtag costume with a bundle of cedar bark for hair on his head. Many times the Hó-e will rid themselves of this personage by pretending to set their hair afire. When Kwikwilyaka mimics this action he actually sets his own hair afire.

Talavai

The Talavai Kachina formerly appeared in pairs on the rooftops and sang songs, waking the people in the village. During the day they would dance with the other kachinas whom they led and prompted in the singing. This role is no longer used in any of the villages. They still appear with the other kachinas in the Powamu Ceremony and are most often standing in a set to one side of the main movement of the procession. Occasionally they sing as they stand holding their spruce trees and ringing their bells. It is unfortunate that the specific name of this kachina is also the generic name of a group of kachinas that appear at dawn on the last day of the Bean Dance and give presents and bean sprouts to the children of the village. This latter group, referred to as Talavai Kachinas may include Huhuwa, Ma'alo, Talavai, Hemis and many others. This is the apearance of the Talavai Kachina as he stands at the side of the procession and sings, except that there would be two of them.

Kwasa-itaka

This kachina is the Hopi form of the Koroasta of the Zuni. Sometimes he is called the Dress Kachina, because he wears a woman's dress without a belt, or the Ota Kachina, from the first words of his song. The most typical feature of the kachina is three little cornhusk packets that make his nose. The lines running around his face are to represent the rainbow colors. He has influence over the growth of corn and carries seeds in the bag in his left hand. Spectators are very eager to receive these seeds and plant them. He is consistently seen in the Third Mesa Powamu. This kachina generally carries sheep scapulae rattles in his right hand, but in recent years this has shifted from the Zuni form to the Hopi rattle. The kachina is supposed to carry a digging stick rather than a cane as represented here.

Huhuwa

Huhuwa is known as the Cross-Legged Kachina
or on First Mesa, the Snare Kachina. Folklore has it that
this kachina is the spirit of a man from Second Mesa,
probably Mishongnovi, who had some crippling disease that
left him barely able to walk. Despite this handicap he
was so cheerful and eager to help others that he still
continues among the Hopi as a kachina. He often appears
as a pair of kachinas hobbling about some village during
a ceremony chattering between themselves. He is
probably chosen more often as a gift-giving kachina
at Powamu times than any other kachina. He is noted for
his remarks which are always humorous. He imitates the
dialects of the various villages and the funny things
the villagers have done. His clothes are always ragged
and give the appearance of having been rescued from
the moths in some Hopi storeroom. Yet he is always
greeted with delight by all who see him. The illustration
shows Huhuwa and Hó-e merging in both appearance
and actions. In recent years there has been an increasing
loss of differentiation between these two personations,
and they may soon merge on some of the mesas.

40

Choshuhuwa

There is no difference between the Bluebird Snare Kachina and the Snare Kachina (Huhuwa) except in the name. The name difference seems to have arisen between First Mesa and Second Mesa but in function and appearance they are the same.

Na-ngasohu Kachina

The Chasing Star or Planet Kachina is a handsome
figure with the enormous fan of eagle plumes behind the
head and the simple but effective design of the face.
Usually he appears in pairs in the Bean Dance Procession,
the Palölökongti, or a Mixed Dance, carrying a bell in
his right hand. His particular function is unknown.

42

Hilili

Hilili is apparently a kachina that has made its way from Acoma or Laguna by a process of osmosis. In these pueblos he is known as Heleleka. By the time he reached the Hopis prior to the turn of the century, his name had changed to Hilili, "from the call that he makes." His first appearance was among the Hopis of First Mesa and the other two mesas made known their disapproval by calling this a witch or Powak Kachina. However, his popularity as a guard kachina and admiration for his rapid dance has increased. Now he is found on all the mesas in a great variety of forms. He appears very frequently in the Powamu and in the Night Dances. This is Hilili as he may appear in a kiva dance. Usually the eyes are not so elaborate, having only a single black line around the eye color. The artist's rendering resembles the Zuni form of Hilili.

Hototo

Hototo appears on all three mesas and on Third
Mesa he is represented by two kachinas. It is quite probable
that this was true of the other two mesas at a point
earlier in time. These kachinas appear most often at the
Bean Dance or Pachavu Ceremony but may also be seen
in the Mixed Dance. They are very important War
Kachinas on Third Mesa, and it is said that the hair
that hangs in place of an ear represents a scalp. The
kachina shown here is the Second Mesa type that is most
often called a Bear Kachina or Tokoch Kachina (Wildcat).
The role he appears in here is as one of the Talavai Kachinas
on the morning of the Bean Dance distributing gifts.

44

Owa-ngazrozro

The Stone Eating Kachina is one of the older Hopi Kachinas and shows great variation between mesas. There appear to be two types currently – one that is seen on First Mesa and at Shungopovi and the other at Mishongnovi and Third Mesa. Each of them has minor variations by village. The kachina may be seen most often in the Powamu. He is one of the Angry Kachinas and is usually led about with a rope around his waist which is held by a Koyemsi; although the rope may also be used to tease this ill-tempered personage. Presumably when rocks are thrown at him he catches them and eats them. On Second Mesa he is primarily a guard and a butt for the antics of the clowns. This illustration shows the kachina as he appears on First Mesa.

Üshe

Üshe is the Hano Cholla Cactus Kachina, a clown
that appears with the Koyemsi at Hano. The Navajo have
a similar figure that goes by the name of Hush-yei or
Chaschin-yei. He carries a long stick with a number of
rolls of piki bread fastened to the end of it. But a piece
of cholla is also on the end of the stick, and the amusement
comes from watching members of the audience attempt
to remove a piece of piki bread without pricking their
fingers. He may also put the fruit of cottonwood trees on
the end of the stick with the same booby trap. This is
not an especially good portrayal of this personage.

46

Situlili

Situlili is a fairly common kachina on Second
Mesa but why he should bear a Zuni name is rather hard to
determine. It is possible that his name refers to tinklers
that he wears on the bottom of his kilt rather than
the Zuni name for rattlesnake. He often appears as
a guard in both the Pachavu and the Powamu Ceremonies.
His actions are characterized by rather sudden
movements followed by pauses as he surveys his
surroundings. Apparently he can come in a variety of
face colors the most common of which are yellow and
brown. The helmet of this kachina is overly large,
but otherwise this is a good portrayal of him; although the
tinklers are not painted in their usual position
on the bottom of the skirt.

Kuwan Kachina

This kachina is described under Ahülani. The artist has drawn Ahülani as he appears during the Soyal but not as he would be seen during the Powamu Ceremony. To be correctly called the Kuwan Kachina he must have a different appearance even though he is the same kachina as Ahülani.

48

Motsin

Motsin, the Disheveled Kachina, is appearing less frequently for his function is to enforce attendance in community work parties. One of the main forms of community work is the cleaning out of the springs, and these have, for the most part been supplanted by water systems. However, he does appear in ceremonies such as the Powamu or Palölökongti. He carries the tools for enforcement of his desires. This kachina can appear in white as shown here, but he is usually black faced. One of the most characteristic marks used to be his appearance in a striped shirt, but over the years the sale of these shirts has disappeared. Now he comes in any convenient shirt. Normally he does not have huzrunkwa (warrior pahos) on top of the head, and the ears nearly always have a fluff of red feathers.

Yo-we

In the late 1600's the Hopis rebelled against
the Spanish priests at the same time as the Pueblos along
the Rio Grande, but in contrast to the eastern groups
the Hopis were never reconquered. Yo-we is thought to
be the kachina that killed the priest at Oraibi during
this revolt. He grabbed for the priest's girl friend but
succeeded only in tearing off one of her earrings, which is
why this kachina always appears with a single earring.
Yo-we is an important Powamu Kachina and never appears
in the ordinary dances such as the Mixed Kachina Dance.
This is the Third Mesa form of Yo-we.

Hano Mana

Hano Mana is given to the girls of Tewa in much the same manner that Hahai-i Wuhti is given the Hopi girls by the men of their villages. Even among the Hopis it is very often a favorite for the first or second gift to the children. She appears in the Bean Dance on Second Mesa and in the Water Serpent Ceremony on First Mesa. Usually if this kachina wears the embroidered wedding robe, it is turned inside out. More often she appears in the maiden shawl. The hair is normally put up in Tewa-style knots on either side of the head rather than as it is shown here. Spruce is held in each hand with the corn.

Nakiachop

The first mention of this kachina is on First Mesa where Stephen (in the 1890's) gives a detailed account of Nakyachop (sic) dancing in the Sio Salako. He is referred to as the Salako Warrior or the Silent Warrior, even though he makes a doleful call. The description is also that of Akush, a Warrior. On Third Mesa, Nakiachop is an Angry Kachina that performed feats of great daring at one of the now deserted villages. In this dance, poles were set into sockets worn into the rock of the mesa edge, and the kachinas danced by climbing the poles and swinging themselves far out over the enormous drop from the rim. The name seems to be the only thing similar between these two kachinas. With the passage of time the division has blurred, and it is possible that what was formerly Siwahop on Third Mesa became Nakiachop and the Akush of First Mesa became Nakiachop, since the Nakiachops of both mesas now look like Talavai. It is possible that this kachina is one that is in the process of becoming extinct. No one agrees on its function, and few can give the correct appearance.

52

Sakwa Hu

Sakwa Hu is an old kachina that has recently appeared with a great deal more frequency on Third Mesa. He is most often portrayed by a small boy and accompanies the procession of the chief kachinas about the village as a guard during the Powamu in February. He is shown here emerging from the kiva to begin his rounds.

PACHAVU CEREMONY

WHEN THE YOUNG MEN of the village are initiated into the various fraternities at the Wuwuchim, an event referred to as the tribal initiation, changes take place in most of the other ceremonies. In the Powamu Ceremony it is the addition of an extra day at the end of the regular ritual. Many kachinas appear *only* in this extended ceremony. Many of the kachinas that are present in the Powamu also appear or may be seen in a different guise at this time. This dramatization occurs at very erratic intervals, and it may not occur for thirty years and then be held again. It never occurs more frequently than every four years.

The content of the Pachavu is basically a dramatization of historical events. On Third Mesa it is the pageant of the advent of the Badger Clan in a Bear Clan village; however there are many overtones of ritual that go far beyond this central theme. One of the more visible events is the vast assemblage of kachinas. Probably the one aspect of the Pachavu Ceremony that remains indelibly fixed in the mind of the viewer is the incredible color of this array of kachinas. Another aspect may be seen in a ritualistic requirement that no one remain outside of the houses or in the village without being under cover when certain ceremonies are performed. At this time the kachinas carry long willow withes that they do not hesitate to use on anyone who does not display great alacrity when entering a house, regardless of whose it is. Once in the house, all doors and windows must be closed against profane viewing of the rites.

Wuwuyomo

The Wuwuyomo are spoken of as "old men kachinas" because they are so ancient. They may also be called Mong Kachina or Chief Kachinas; in fact on Third Mesa this is the only name by which they are now known. They always appear in groups of four with the Pachavu Manas in the extended form of the Powamu Ceremony on Third Mesa. There they lead the manas into the village. An important part of this ritual is pausing along the processional route to sing songs that are important to the growth of the crops in the coming year. The Wuwuyomo also appear in the procession in the Palölökong or Water Serpent Ceremony and afterward as a group in one of the kivas where they sing. Formerly on First Mesa they appeared with the Sio Salako, but this has changed through the years; and apparently they no longer come with this Zuni-inspired group. Wuwuyomo is characterized by the Soyal pahos on the head and the scapulae in the right hand and the lack of tinklers on the long stockings.

Pachavu Hú

Four of these kachinas appear during the Powamu and inspect the bean plants on the last four days of the Powamu Ceremony. It is their duty to guard the bean plants, and if they are damaged, they may whip all members of the offending kiva. Likewise they check to see that no members of the kivas are lying down. If they are, it may adversely affect the growth of the beans, and that would be a poor omen for the approaching season. As everyone desires the coming season of growth to be a success, they try to make the bean crop in the kiva as perfect as possible. It is unfortunate that the artist did not choose to paint this kachina as a group rather than as a single kachina. This is the Third Mesa variety of this personage.

56

Hé-é-e

Hé-é-e or Hé'wuhti may be seen in Powamu celebrations most years, but it is at the Pachavu ceremonies that Hé-é-e is seen in her most impressive appearance. This kachina is the Warrior Maid, based on the story of a young girl. Many years ago, tradition says that some Hopis were living outside of the main village, and the mother of this household was putting up her daughter's hair. The mother had finished only one side of the hair whorls, the hair on the other side still hanging loosely, when they saw enemies sneaking toward the village. The daughter snatched up a bow, quiver and arrows from the wall and raced toward the village to warn the people. She then led the defense until the men in the fields could return and rout the enemy. She has been personated ever since as a kachina and always appears with her hair partially up on one side and hanging down on the other. On the back of her head she wears an artifical scalp lock, and she carries the weapons she snatched up so long ago. She still guards the village. During Pachavu times she gives the signal that drives everyone indoors when certain ceremonies must be performed out in the open. And it is she who leads the horde of hooting, jangling, threatening kachinas along the line of procession into the village in the final moments of the ceremony of Pachavu. This is a good illustration of Hé-é-e; although the figure should wear his quiver on the other shoulder unless he is left handed. Also, the arms should be whitened, and there should be cornhusk crosses on the cape of the kachina.

Pachavuin Mana

This is the only instance where the masked kachina figure is truly a woman. In appearance she resembles the Kachin Mana that accompanies the Hemis Kachina, but the Kachin Mana is a man. Pachavuin Mana is a woman. These kachinas bring the bean sprouts into the village during the Pachavu Ceremony. After they assemble at a shrine the bean sprouts are brought to them while Hé-é-e is keeping the villagers from watching the harvest. A multitude of kachinas also gather near the shrine, and a procession is formed. Usually it is led by the Powamu Chief, and followed in order by other chiefs, the Chief Kachinas, and the Pachavuin Manas and their helpers. The entire procession is totally surrounded by a horde of guards and whippers, and the group moves steadily toward the village. Upon their arrival they make a ceremonial circuit of the Chief Kiva and perform certain rites. Then at a given signal, the eyes of the uninitiated are covered, and within seconds the entire crowd of kachinas disappears, leaving only the stately Chief Kachinas and the Village Chiefs. This painting is a representation of the Pachavuin Mana as she appears on Second Mesa. However, the tray that she carries has been given a stylistic treatment; for the actual tray is filled to a height of nearly two feet and is nearly as broad. The enormous mound of bean sprouts has beanpods, artificial corn, corn sprouts and grass in it.

58

Tanakwewa

Colton states that this kachina is very important on Second Mesa during the Bean Dance in initiation years or Pachavu times, and this may be so. The only time that I have seen this kachina was in the morning procession of the Pachavu at Mishongnovi, and I was unable to discover what function he performs.

Hahai-i Wuhti

This is one of the more colorful of the Hopi kachinas. She is present in many ceremonies, Salako, Powamu, Pachavu, Palölökongti, and even the Soyoko. Her personality is that of a sprightly Hopi grandmother. She may be found speaking in her shrill falsetto for the Nataskas on First Mesa. She would be demanding meat for them, for after all they are her and Chaveyo's children. Failing to get the kind or quantity of meat desired, she may be heard berating the inconsiderate, hard-hearted individuals and muttering dire threats. Again she may be seen in the Salako exhorting those giant bird-like kachinas through an elaborate ritual. In yet another guise she appears in the Third Mesa Pachavu offering the children somiviki, a Hopi food, and when they reach for it she pours water on their heads. This is not an idle act but one with ceremonial meaning. And at yet another time she will be seen as the wet nurse of the Water Serpents during the Puppet Dances. Wherever she appears she is usually very vocal, an attribute not common among the other kachinas. In addition to being the mother of the monsters, she is thought of as mother of dogs, and of kachinas. It is her tihu or doll that is given to the very young Hopi babies and captive eagles. This is more or less the appearance of Hahai-i as she appears on Third Mesa. The Third Mesa form usually has a black carrying shawl across her back and over her arms in front as a strap.

Palakwayo

It would be logical for the Red-tailed Hawk to be simply another Bird Kachina, but logic plays little part in understanding kachinas. Palakwayo is one of the Chief Kachinas of Second Mesa during Pachavu of initiation years. He appears as one of the more important kachinas on Third Mesa during the Powamu, but his function is unknown. He has almost disappeared in some villages, but countless shrines still exist that were his. During the Pachavu at Oraibi he is one of the group that Hé-é-e gathers for her procession into the village. The artist has portrayed him as a brown-faced eagle which is not his usual appearance. He is generally rather plain.

Söhönasomtaka

Despite the fact that a great many Hopi have
never heard of this kachina she is a very important warrior
woman from Old Oraibi. When Hé-é-e makes her swing
by to pick up kachina guards for the Pachavu Ceremony,
the second stop she makes is at the shrine of this
kachina. She is a very ancient kachina and a very powerful
one in warfare, closely allied with Masau'u. She appears
only at Oraibi. The artist chose to put spruce in the
hands of this kachina rather than the bow and arrows
that she usually carries as one of the "Angry" or
War Kachinas.

62

Ewiro

Ewiro is an old style Third Mesa Kachina that normally appears during Pachavu. However, he may appear to make war on the clowns during the regular plaza dances later in the year. He functions as a policeman and formerly oversaw the cleaning out of springs. The small shield that this kachina carries may be barely discerned at his right side. The smudge in the illustration on the right side of the beard is an abortive attempt at a ruff. The correct type of ruff is shown on the left side of the beard.

Tumoala

The Devil's Claw Kachina is named for *Martynia louisiana* or Devil's Claw, a plant that grows on the Hopi Reservation. It usually appears after the rains come and grows with a rather dense green foliage. It is felt that the Devil's Claw can hold the clouds, and so it is used as a kachina. This kachina appears in the Pachavu Ceremony and also in the Mixed Kachina Dances. In the illustration the artist has depicted the real plant along the brim of the kachina's mask. However, when the kachina appears, he has blue hook-shaped artificial pods in the same position but does not use the real plant.

64

KACHINA CULT INITIATION CEREMONY

AT THE TIME of the Powamu, another short ceremony occurs: the initiation of the young children into the Kachina Cult. This is the time when the youngsters are told that the kachinas are not actual spirits but the men of their village assuming a spiritual identity. The actual ceremony is not complex by Hopi standards. It embodies the indoctrination of the children in certain esoteric lore. Usually a sand painting altar and a ceremonial whipping of the children are included along with the appearance of three kachinas: the Crow Mother and her two sons the Hú or Tungwup Kachinas. There are several other subsidiary kachinas that may appear on certain mesas, and the Powamu Kachinas are always a part of the ceremony even though they appear later.

Angwusnasomtaka

Angwusnasomtaka (the Crow Mother) is a figure
of great dignity. She appears on all three mesas, usually in
connection with the initiation of the children, although
she also appears on other occasions. At the initiation rites
she descends into the kiva bearing a large number of
yucca blades bound together at the base. She takes a
position at one corner of the large sand painting on the
floor of the kiva, with one of her "sons" on either side
of her. As the candidate is brought to the sand painting
she hands a whip to one of the Hú Kachinas who gives
the child four healthy strokes with the yucca blade.
When the yucca becomes worn it is handed back to the
Crow Mother who then supplies a new one. When the
initiatory whipping is over, she raises her skirts and
receives the same treatment accorded the children. They are
then given prayer feathers and meal and leave the kiva.
On some mesas she is referred to as Angwushahai-i
because she talks, thus confusing her with the Crow
Bride.

Hú

When the time approaches for whipping the children during ceremonies in the kiva, a signal is given and the three kachinas: the Crow Mother and her two sons, the Hú Kachinas, come rushing toward the kiva. There they make four circuits of the hatchway creating as much noise as possible by beating the hatchway with their whips and bounding about to make their rattles sound. At the end of the fourth circuit they enter the kiva and take their positions north of the fireplace. The initiates are brought forward by their ceremonial god-parents and placed on the sand painting. The Hú Kachinas advance and give them four strokes with their yucca whips. As each candidate is struck the yucca whip is waved through the air with a wicked swish. This is a gesture of purification. After the Hú Kachinas finish whipping the children, they whip each other and then the Crow Mother. The Kachina Chief then dismisses them with prayer feathers and cornmeal. They depart as noisily as they came. The artist has drawn the kachina as he approaches to deliver a stroke and the sight is indeed a horrifying one. However, the figure should have his lower legs as well as his lower arms painted white, rather than as shown in this illustration.

Qalavi

Qalavi is the kachina who holds the initiates
during their ceremonial whipping at Powamu on Second
Mesa. He appears only on Second Mesa. He is usually
portrayed carrying yucca-leaf whips, but in this illustration
he is in his ritual pose. Normally the eyes are not shown
at all in this kachina or, if shown, they are blue rings
as is the mouth. In addition, this kachina should
appear naked with the exception of the blue belt.
He never wears a kilt.

Ongchoma

Ongchoma is presumed to be a very compassionate kachina who sympathizes with the children about to be whipped during the Powamu initiation. He carries a mano and touches them with it to make them hard so they will not feel the whip. The kachina portrayed here is exactly the same as A-ha with the exception of the filled-in cheek marks (hachures).

Chowilawu

Chowilawu is a kachina that few Hopi men will
make as a doll. Very few can be found and they are in the
older collections. Reverend Voth (a Mennonite missionary
among the Hopis in the 1890's) managed to persuade
someone to make a doll of this kachina, for which they
were both roundly castigated by the priests of Oraibi.
The kachina appears during the initiation into the Powamu
fraternity, an event that usually takes place the day
before the initiation into the Kachina cult. He is never
seen in public, even though he appears on all three mesas.
Some Hopis equate this kachina with Qöchaf and others
with the whirlwind, but it seems doubtful that he is
either of these. If this kachina did not have a ruff and
if its lower legs and forearms were blackened, it would
be a closer representation of this particular personation.
The black spot on its chest is matched by one on its
back, but the spots should not be encircled; rather they
are a small smudge just over the sternum and in the
same position on the back.

70

Powamu Kachina

The Powamu Kachinas are always portrayed with a mask, whether they appear in the plaza or in the form of paintings or dolls. However, the most common appearance of the actual dancer is without a mask for the simple reason that the Powamu Kachinas are the first to show the newly initiated youngsters that they are just people portraying the spirits. I am sure this is one of the reasons that these kachinas dance so late at night. The vast majority of the Powamu dancers come in a group divided almost equally between men and "women". The men are dressed as kachinas but do not wear masks, and are replete with jewelry, costume and paint. Together with the women they perform their unusual dance, one that resembles a square dance. Not all are Powamu Kachinas. Thus at the same ceremony it is possible to see several varieties of kachinas both with and without masks. This Powamu Kachina is shown masked as he should be, for it is not proper that the uninitiated see kachinas, particularly such important ones, without masks.

71

Powamu So-aum

In actuality this is a group of kachinas and not
a single personation and would probably be more correctly
called the Powamu Manam. Appearing with the Powamu
Kachinas are a great variety of female personations.
The normal group of dancers will be composed about
equally of men and "women". The "women" may appear
as any kind of female the men choose, and thus mini-
skirted Anglos appear with demure Rio Grande
girls, and Navajo with Negro. Child and grandmother all
parade down the ladder into the kiva with their faces
dimly seen through a strategically held spruce bough.
As each one goes down, a falsetto voice from overhead
describes in too much detail the shortcomings of the
"woman" who is descending. When at last the owner of
the voice descends, she is usually an old, hag-like
grandmother, white-faced and scraggly-haired. She is the
Powamu So-aum, the Powamu Grandmother. The figure
drawn by the artist is that of the Powamu So-aum as she
appeared in a Powamu Dance on First Mesa over seventy
years ago. She still appears like this.

72

SOYOKO CEREMONY

EARLY IN THE Bean Dance time (Powamu) the young children of the villages can expect a visit from the terrifying figure of Soyok Wuhti and a couple of her ugly helpers. These individuals go from house to house where there are small children and leave a token and a warning with each child. Every girl is given a small amount of sweet corn and told to grind lots of cornmeal. The boys are presented with yucca snares and told to catch mice because the Soyoko are coming again in four days, and when they appear they will want meat and food or they will take the youngsters instead. When the Ogres do appear they present themselves in horrid array in front of a house and demand food and meat. It is held out to them on the end of a stick from behind a partially closed door. It will be instantly rejected as too little or the wrong kind, and the child is demanded. With chilling detail the falsetto voice of the Soyoko then recounts faithfully the child's misdeeds and demands to be given the youngster. At this point some relative usually speaks up for the child saying that he or she has really learned not to do these things. But the Ogre is adamant and the child may have to demonstrate that he minds his parents and doesn't spill the water or whatever. This is done for the edification of the Ogres and the audience which stays well back from these ugly creatures. Finally the child will be ransomed with quantities of food which are dumped in the burden baskets on the backs of the Heheya, We-u-u, or the Toson Koyemsi. They trot off to the officiating kiva with their loads and then return for still more.

When all of the houses in the village have been visited, the Soyoko return to the kiva where they find a dance in progress. This dance is a Butterfly or similar performance. Lured by the dance and the blandishments of the kiva chief, they join the dancers with hilarious results. The Soyok Wuhti stands aloof from this frivolity, and when members of her horde attempt to join the dance, she knocks them about with the butt of her cane. But growing more and more excited the Heheya attempt to peer under the skirts of the young boys who perform as the women in the dance group. Amazingly the dance proceeds with almost no break in the rhythm. The kiva chief finally succeeds in enticing the Soyok Wuhti into the dance where she makes the most ludicrous mistakes, turning a half-turn too late or attempting to dance with the wrong foot. Her actions convulse the audience with laughter. While she is completely occupied by the dancing with the chief, the men of the kiva suddenly leap upon all these evil creatures and divest them of their ill-gotten gains, rushing into the kiva with the food. The last that is seen of the Soyoko is Soyok Wuhti rushing empty-armed and half-naked over the edge of the mesa.

Soyok Wuhti

The awesome figure of the Monster Woman appears
during the Powamu ceremony as one of the many Soyoko
who threaten the lives of the children. Dressed all in
black, with long straggling hair, staring eyes and a
wide-fanged mouth, she carries a blood-smeared knife
and a long jangling crook — a truely fearsome creature to
the children. When she speaks, it is in a wailing falsetto or
with a long dismal hoot of "Soyoko'-u-u-u," from
which her name is derived. She may reach for the children
with the long crook and threaten to put them in the
basket on her back, or to cut off their heads with the
large knife that she carries in her hand utterly terrifying
her young audience. On some mesas she may be the
ogre that threatens a small child who has been
naughty and bargains with a relative to ransom the
child, but on others she is not. In some villages she leads
the procession of ogres; in others she remains at the side,
content to make threatening gestures. This is the First Mesa
Soyok Wuhti, or Monster Woman, with several changes
incorporated from the normal appearance. The
blood-stained hands are lacking, and the crook is a
short one. Usually the crook is almost seven feet long with
tinklers on it. On First Mesa ragged, brown, high
moccasins are used in place of the woman's white boot.
Tufts of cotton are stuck in her hair, and the general
appearance is one of darkness and dirtiness.

Awatovi Soyok Wuhti

The Awatovi Ogre Woman is
exactly like Soyok Wuhti except that she is believed
to have come from the destroyed pueblo of
Awatovi. Formerly she appeared more frequently
on First Mesa. She behaves as Soyok Wuhti does when she
stands by the side of the kachina who is speaking,
scraping her saw on the building and reaching for
unwary spectators or children. Usually this individual
has a mat of wool for the hair on the mask, surmounted by
a red feather. The mask seldom has red ears, being
one of the few that does not.

Awatovi Soyok Taka

The Awatovi Monster Man performs the
same function as do the Nataska. His role is almost
exactly that of Wiharu, the white Nataska. He stands beside
the Soyok Wuhti and puts food in his basket that she
gathers from the villagers. He is believed to have
come from the destroyed town of Awatovi and is seldom
personated. Usually this kachina wears a black
breechclout rather than the more elaborate embroidered
kilt. In addition the calves and forearms are covered with
black spots but are otherwise unpainted.

76

Soyok Mana

Appearing in the company of her towering brothers, the Nataska Mana or Soyok Mana comes during the Powamu ceremony. Usually she will be found close to Nataska's Uncle, and when food is offered to her that does not satisfy the Ogre's wants, she whistles in disapproval. She carries only the large burden basket into which she puts any acceptable food. The artist's version of this kachina is rather different from that usually seen, for the Nataska Mana or Soyok Mana has neither a wide mouth nor a big beard, and she carries nothing in her hands. She is not a leader, but is essentially one of the figures used to carry the spoils back to the kiva.

Nataska

The fearsome Nataska always come as a pair. They accompany the Soyoko on their collection trip and usually stand directly behind the member of their crew who is bargaining with the relatives of the children. They make horrible noises, dragging their saws along the side of the house or on the ground. All the while, they keep up a steady stamping that makes the turtle-shell rattles on their legs sound ominously. They are supposed to be able to eat a child whole; from the very earliest age, the child has heard stories of these monsters — how they would descend on children playing near the village and haul them away to cook and eat. So it is no wonder that the children are petrified at their actual appearance! Usually only dark-colored clothes are put on this kachina pair, who should have horns. The feather fan is made of turkey feathers which are placed close together to form a large mass behind the head that makes the figures appear much taller and broader. Also the wide belt will be stained red.

78

Tahaum Soyoko

Accompanying the Nataska is Tahaum Soyoko, their uncle, who resembles them in many ways. While Soyok Wuhti tells those assembled at a given household that they will cut off their heads or fling them over the cliff and hunt them down, the Nataska and Tahaum Soyoko maintain a constant prancing step and brandish their weapons making horrible noises. The artist has put a Chaveyo headdress on this kachina rather than the solid radiating fan of feathers at the back of the head. The mouth is not made to open and the kachina's appearance is considerably changed by this interpretation.

Wiharu

The White Ogre or Wiharu performs in exactly the same manner that the Nataska do and differs only in color.

Toson Koyemsi

A number of these kachinas used to come with the Soyoko on Third Mesa and demand sweet cornmeal from the girls. They would then sit and taste the cornmeal to see if it was well-ground and sweet, and from this comes their name of Sweet Cornmeal Tasting Koyemsi. Since the Soyoko has not been performed on Third Mesa for over half a century, this kachina no longer appears in this role, part of which is now played by Heheya Aumutaka, on Third Mesa. He does not appear on First Mesa, and the Second Mesa form is radically different. This is the most common appearance of the Third Mesa Toson Koyemsi. He appears early in the morning on the final day of Powamu and delivers presents and bean sprouts to individuals about the village. Most often these presents are for children, but they can just as easily be for adults.

Heheya Kachin Mana

This Kachin Mana is rather common on First Mesa but progressively less so on Second and Third Mesas. She usually accompanies the Nataskas on their collecting trip around First Mesa and occasionally on Second Mesa. When food is offered that is inferior, or is not offered at all, she whistles and attempts to rope the delinquents to drag them away in lieu of the food. She does not appear in the Powamu but rather with the Soyoko. The mana is shown here in the act of roping some poor individual who has not produced the proper food. Normally she wears a blouse under the woman's dress so that the juncture of the mask with the neck is hidden.

Heheya Aumutaka

This is the Third Mesa Heheya Aumutaka, and he appears only on that Mesa. There are other forms on First and Second Mesa. Formerly he accompanied the Soyoko when they appeared on Third Mesa but since the Soyoko no longer come, his role is shifting to that of a general Powamu Kachina. This is a very good illustration of this kachina whose name means "like Heheya" rather than "Heheya's Uncle."

NIGHT DANCES

DANCES ARE HELD in the kivas during the months of winter and early spring. These Night Dances, when held before Powamu (Bean Dance), are called Pamuya (January) Dances as this is the month in which they occur. Those that are held after Powamu are known as the Ankwati or Anktioni, the Repeat Dances. All are called Night Dances or Kiva Dances. Second Mesa does not present kachina performances during Pamuya but the other mesas will have kachinas such as the Zuni personations that appear on First Mesa at this time. All three mesas present Repeat Dances and it is during this time that many interesting but lesser ceremonies occur. There is considerable variation between the mesas as to the type of dance that may be held during this period. The Palölökong Dance is held in this interval on First Mesa where it has a set place in the ceremonial cycle. However, it occurs only sporadically on Third Mesa and not at all on Second Mesa. Third Mesa may in addition present a Puppet Dance featuring the Salako and Palhik Manas with the Water Serpent. This particular performance does not seem to occur on either First or Second Mesa. Third Mesa also presents the Palhik Dance that is personated entirely by men in distinction to the other mesas where the dance is given by women and is not considered to be a kachina performance. The Salako may appear in Third Mesa kivas during this period but apparently does not on either First or Second Mesa. One other dance that appears with some regularity on all three mesas is that of the Barter Kachinas or Huyan. This is a generic term for a number of kachinas that may take part in this physically demanding performance. During these Night Dances many kachinas may be seen for there is a vast reservoir of kachinas that may be called upon to dance. The Pamuya seems to use a great variety of bird of Zuni kachinas. Almost any of the kachinas that appear in the Mixed or Ordinary Dances may be personated at times in the Night Dances.

Momo

The Bee makes rather casual appearances during the Mixed Kachina Dances or during the night rituals of the Water Serpent Ceremony. He presumably dances among the audience, although how anyone could dance through the tightly packed humanity is hard to imagine. With a tiny bow and miniature arrows he either threatens to shoot the spectators or actually does hit some of them with tiny blunt arrows. In Zuni, when this personation appears, he brings honey to the children in the audience in the odd-shaped cups that appear on the top of his head. I doubt that the Bee Kachina would dare shoot any members of the audience with the lethal-looking bow and arrow that the artist has shown. It is usually a miniature rather than one this large.

Tatangaya

The striped form of the Hornet or Wasp Kachina may be a recent borrowing from the Zuni. There are two distinct types of Tatangaya, and this one seems to be the most recent. He comes in groups or singly during the Pamuya or the Mixed Kachina Dances. There are many examples of this kachina in older collections of dolls and they are bright and colorful. Recently, however, there has not been quite as much interest in the Wasp Kachina. This is an excellent rendering of this kachina.

Kwahu

Occasionally in one of the night ceremonies in March or during the Powamu one may have the satisfaction of seeing a performance of the Eagle Kachina. Usually the personator imitates the step or motion and cry of the eagle to absolute perfection. There is evidence that this kachina was imported into Zuni from the Hopi and is danced there in much the same manner that it is at Hopi. This may be why the Eagle may appear during Pamuya on First Mesa with Zuni Kachinas. This is a recent form of the Eagle. Third Mesa formerly had an eagle with an all-black body to which bits of eagle down were stuck with pitch. The headdress is not as it appears on First Mesa, and on Second Mesa the body is very frequently painted yellow and red.

Turposkwa

The Canyon Wren Kachina is another of the many bird personations that are performed in the Kiva Dances. These Kiva Dances occur in Pamuya, Powamuya, or Ankwati. In earlier times the Wren was a runner on Third Mesa, but from the costume that the artist has shown it would of necessity be a kiva performance. The bird on his head represents a wren. The costume of this kachina consists of two sashes, the ends of which hang down in front and behind. He does not wear a kilt and a rattle should be in his right hand and in his left, a branch.

Tocha

The Hummingbird (Tocha) is a favorite kiva group impersonation. Sometime during the Bean Dance, and presumably during the Soyal, a number of these brilliant figures will appear. As they enter the kiva they bob, give a sharp call and then proceed to dance with great rapidity. This particular kachina appears very often as a runner, but the artist has chosen to show him as he appears during the Kiva Dances in the winter ceremonies.

Yapa

The Mockingbird Kachina (Yapa) appears in the Night Dances of the Pamuya or Powamuya — a time when bird impersonations seem to be favored. He is rather different in appearance on all three mesas, but all seem to have the same folktale that it was he who taught women to speak. This is a good illustration.

90

Mongwa Wuhti

This kachina, the Great Horned Owl Woman, is most uncommon. In fact almost all versions of it may be traced back to one reference. It is not generally known by the Hopis. Most will say that it is a possibility as a kachina and maybe someone could do it that way. This figure is shown in Fewkes' article on Hopi Kachinas and appears nowhere else. The drawing here is of the same First Mesa Kachina that is shown in Fewkes and described in Colton.

Hotsko

The Screech Owl is another of the many birds that may appear during the Kiva Dances of the Powamu or before. He is not supposed to appear on Third Mesa nor Second, but this may be a case of "very seldom" rather than "never." There are strong evidences of acculturation in the kachina's hunting for he has not taken a wild duck but instead has got into someone's barnyard and taken a domestic duck. From the expression on his face it must have been an unpleasant encounter.

Salap Mongwa

The role of the Spruce Owl is unclear, but it seems safe to assume that it resembles that of Mongwa. However, in various sources this kachina does not carry the kind of paraphernalia shown. He has spruce tucked into armlets and under a black breechclout and belt. He also holds spruce in the left hand and a rattle in the right. This is not the mark of the Warrior Kachinas; just what his role may be awaits additional information.

Kowako

This kachina, the Chicken, is definitely post-Spanish and, in all probability, does not date much before 1850, as the Hopi did not have chickens until quite late. Nevertheless there are folktales about the Chicken and how he lost his girl friend to the Mockingbird Kachina. He appears most often in the kivas during the Palölökong or during the winter Kiva Dances. He may also appear during the dances of early spring in the plaza. Most of the appearances seem to have a strong element of the comic in them as though this kachina may have started as a piptuka. This is a much more believable representation of the Chicken Kachina than the one illustrated in Fewkes (1900:Pl. XVIII). However, the kachina illustrated should possibly be called Takawea rather that Kowako for it is most definitely a Rooster.

Buffalo Kachina

In appearance the Buffalo Kachina is the same as the Buffalo Dancer with the following exception: he is always masked. The mask has a snout and globular eyes as well; thus the Buffalo "Kachina" shown in Fewkes is not the kachina form but the dancer form. The Buffalo Kachina is performed, as are most of the game animal kachinas, as a prayer for the increase of that particular animal. The dance is usually held right after the kachina return in the winter and is given in the kivas. The dance does not usually incorporate any female impersonators or women as the Social Dance does. The Buffalo Kachina is shown in the usual dancing position holding a lightning stick and rattle. He is dressed as the Second Mesa Buffalo Dancer.

95

Saviki

The name of this kachina changes from mesa to mesa. As Tcanau, one of the old ones of the Bakab (Reed) Clan at First Mesa, he appears during the March ceremonies, or during the Ankwati when the Water Serpent is carried down to the spring for certain rites. In this role Tcanau appears as four individuals who are guardians for the Palölökong. His role on Second Mesa is unknown, but on Third Mesa he again appears as a guardian. Under the name of Saviki he is one of the Bow Clan ancients and appears as a single individual with Tangik'china and two Kokoshoya when the Salako comes in person during Ankwati. The snake that the kachina carries in his mouth is a bull snake, and generally there is a lizard above his eyes. He does not have globular eyes or teeth in his snout.

Kana-a Kachina

The Kana-a Kachina is also the Sunset Crater Kachina, and the Crater itself, near Flagstaff, is quite often called Kana-a Kachinki or the house of Kana-a Kachina. The actual name of this kachina is much closer to Ka'ana but has reached print as Kana or Kana-a. Since the latter name appears in common use it should be retained. Legend has it that this is the kachina who danced at one of the ancient villages and started Sunset Crater. He does not appear in the regular kachina dances, only at night or on special occasions. Usually this kachina wears a kilt made of a rabbit skin rug as was his cape. He also wears a wide embroidered sash tied at the right, and a bandolier from which is hung many ears of roasted corn. The face is usually blue and yellow with the dividing line in the other direction.

Sio Hemis Ta-amu

The Zuni Hemis Kachina's Uncle comes with the Sio Hemis whenever he appears. He may be seen in the kachina's return in Pamuya or during a Sio Hemis Niman Ceremony, but he is not a common kachina. Dolls are occasionally made of him, but they are rare. The representation here is very close to that of the illustration in Fewkes (1900:Pl.V).

Chakwaina

This kachina was brought from Zuni by the Asa Clan when they came to Sichomovi. Since that time he has spread to the other mesas. However, Chakwaina originally came from much farther east for he has homologues in Keresan and Tanoan pueblos along the Rio Grande. It has been stated that this kachina represents Estevan the Moor, who led Fray Marcos de Niza in search of Cibola and was killed at Zuni. This does not seem too reasonable considering the direction of his diffusion and the complex relationship of the Chakwaina group to the various pueblos where it is found. Chakwaina appears most often in January during the Kiva Dances — dancing in a line with rather lively gestures, stooping and turning and singing a spirited tune. All Chakwaina are warriors. This figure is essentially correct in detail but does not capture the true appearance of the kachina. In recent years there has been an increasing tendency to put a star on one cheek and a moon on the other, a feature formerly reserved for the Chakwaina side dancer.

Chakwaina Sho-adta

It is a little difficult to explain how one can be their own grandmother but this is the case with Chakwaina Sho-adta and Chakwaina Mana. They are one and the same kachina. The confusion arises in the fact that the Asa Clan is also called the Chakwaina Clan and one of their most revered kachinas is Chakwaina Mana. Chakwaina Mana is the "grandmother" of the Chakwaina Clan, their old war chief and also clan ancient. Her story is exactly the same as that of Hé-é-e, in that in a state of undress she managed to help turn the enemy and was consequently made a kachina. Her appearance is also that of Hé-é-e with very minor differences, and she cannot be differentiated except by context. She appears with the Chakwaina when they dance.

100

Koroasta

Koroasta, Koroista, or Korosta, is a Rio Grande Keresan Kachina where his name is Akorosta. He appears at Zuni, and he appears on First Mesa more than the other Hopi mesas. He carries a planting stick and seeds, and he dances in the kiva just as does Kwasaitaka, who is the Third Mesa form of this kachina. He is supposed to have influence over the growth of corn and most often carries corn kernels in his sack. The audience is anxious to receive any of this seed corn that he cares to pass out. Sometimes this kachina is called Ota from the first words of his song.

Patszro

The Snipe Kachina appears in the Kiva Dances before and after the important Powamu Ceremony. His function is probably the same as that of all the other bird kachinas who make their appearance at this time. With a few exceptions this is a good representation of the Snipe Kachina.

102

Hospoa

The Roadrunner Kachina appears either during the nighttime Kiva Dances or during the Mixed Kachina Dances later in the spring. He does not appear as often as formerly, but occasionally dolls are made of him. This kachina nearly always comes with a moisture tablet on his back. (A moisture tablet is a painted, flat, rectangular object to solicit rain.)

Koyona

The Turkey Kachina appears with the other birds in the kivas at night or during the Mixed Dances of late spring. He is not a common kachina and seems to be only from First Mesa.

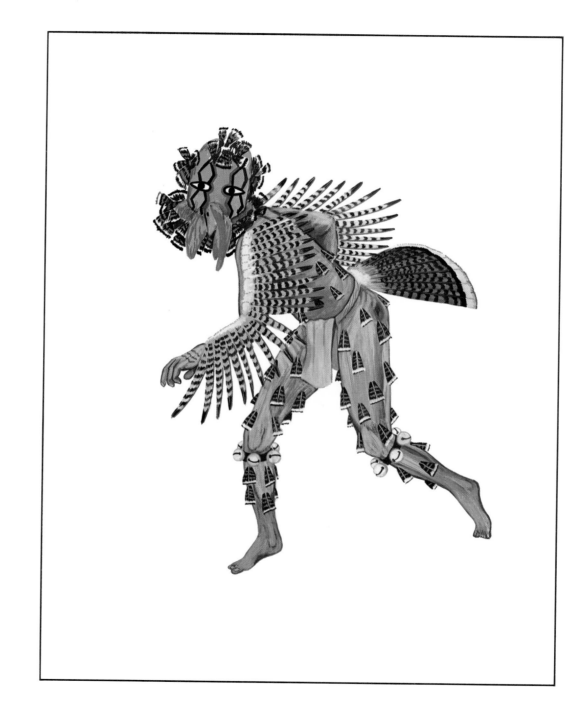

Poli Kachina

The Poli or Butterfly Kachina and his partner always appear together but only in the kiva during the Night Dance. The Poli Kachina is the male form of the Poli Mana, and in a reverse of the usual, he is less well-known than the Mana. He seems to appear solely on Third Mesa and may actually be a development of that Mesa. His partner looks almost exactly like the Palhik Mana, but does not serve quite the same function. This female kachina partner is portrayed by a man unlike the regular Palhik Mana who is a woman. The steps and postures of the Poli Kachina and Mana, in fact the entire form of the dance, are very much like that of the more common social Butterfly Dance. The figure is shown without the pavaiyokyasi, or moisture tablet, that usually adorns the back of this kachina.

Palhik Mana

The figure of the Palhik Mana is one of the most deceptive of all Hopi Kachinas. Probably it is best to think of this kachina as a continuum beginning with the simple Poli Mana at one end and finishing with the Hopi Salako Mana at the other. Somewhere in between lies the Palhik Mana. This hypothetical continuum relates only to appearance. The functions of the personation vary in direct ratio to the similarity of appearance. As Poli Mana she is the dancing companion to the Poli Kachina of Third Mesa and is personated by a man. As Salako Mana she is either the partner of the towering Salako Taka or the maid who grinds corn during the Puppet Dances in the kivas. When she grinds corn as does the Salako Mana, the only difference lies in the vari-colored eyes of the Salako Mana. If Palhik Mana dances, she does so in quite a different manner than does the Poli Mana, and on First and Second Mesa she is portrayed by women. As such she is not considered a kachina, but on Third Mesa she appears masked and is portrayed by men. However, if a Hopi is asked to define the difference between Salako Mana and Palhik Mana he will usually reply that they are the same, the Corn Grinding Girls — two facets of a single concept. The name Palhik is probably derived from the fact that the women drink a very thin gruel as food when they dance during the Mamzrau Ceremonial. If the Palhik Mana does not appear in person during this ceremony, she may be present as pictures on the marauvaho carried in the hands of the celebrants. To further complicate the situation, the Butterfly Dancer who appears in one version of the social dance is very close in appearance to Poli Mana and Palhik Mana.

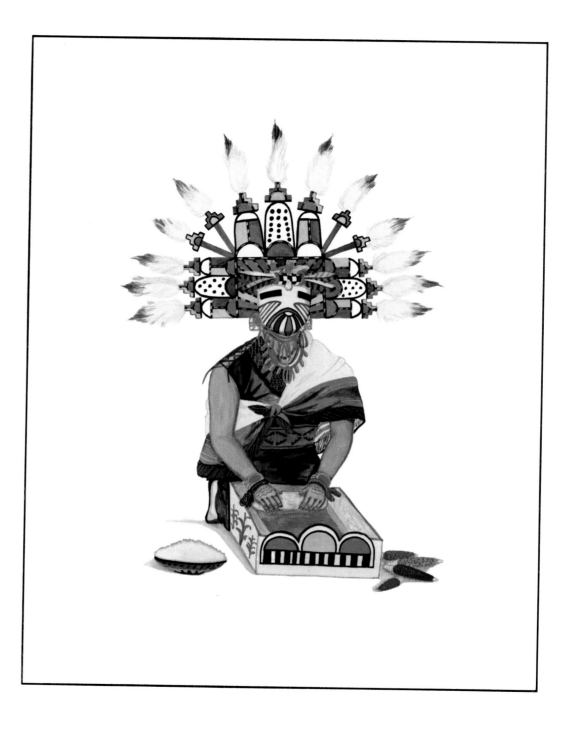

WHEN THE WEATHER warms and the Ankwati or Anktioni Dances draw to a close, kachina dances are held in the plaza of the village. These dances may be either Mixed Kachina Dances (Soyohim) where all of the dancers are different types of kachinas, or they may be a dance where all of the kachinas are the same — the Regular or Line Dance. Fewkes refers to these as the abbreviated kachina dances for they do not have the elaborate ceremonialism that accompanies the more important rites such as the Powamu or Niman. The dances may be sponsored by people who wish to commemorate some special event such as the return of a son from the army, the recovery from an illness, or a child's birthday. While there is always a strong element of religion present in these dances; there is also an equally strong element of entertainment. New songs appear, and as any popular song would be, these are recorded and played for days after the dances. Feasts are held and neighbors visit one another; a constant parade of guests, both invited and fortuitous, pass from house to house as the dancers make their periodic appearances in the plaza. There are often clowns to entertain the audience between dances in the afternoon. Sometimes these clowns are part of an organized group, but they may be impromptu performers that sweep the assembled with gales of laughter. These events are great enjoyment for all, and their presentation is very dear to the hearts of all Hopis. Each of the kachinas presented in one of these dances has a definite purpose, often in addition to their primary purpose of bringing rain and fertility. Most of these kachinas are not limited to the Plaza Dances but may also be presented during the earlier Night Dances or during the procession of the Bean Dance. They are most commonly seen in the Plaza Dances. In this section the kachinas from Ösök'china to Heoto Mana are Mixed Dancers, and those from Kuwan Heheya through Sio Kachina form the Line Dancers.

Ösök'china

Ösök'china is an enforcer. He may appear in the Mixed Kachina Dance or as a single individual who rousts out the laggards when there is work to be done. He usually wears cactus on the crown of his head and may also carry it in his hand. If he appears in the Mixed Kachina Dances he usually carries a rattle in his right hand. The decoration on his cheeks is the cactus flower or the outline of the cactus itself. This kachina probably should not have a burden basket on his back nor have I seen any representation with the black band over the eyes in this manner.

108

Kokopelli

Undoubtedly Kokopelli, the Hump-backed Flute Player, has caught the imagination of more people than any other Hopi kachina except perhaps the Hemis Kachina. Some of that interest is because he is so blatantly phallic in nature, but beyond this he appears in every nook and cranny of the Southwest. His image is found in all of the pueblos and among the southern Indians as well. He dances happily around a Hohokam pot and chases mountain sheep through the canyons of the San Juan. There is always speculation about what inspired this particular personation. Ties with Mexico and even South America have been suggested for he appears in all of these places. Among the Hopis he is a Flute Player only when he borrows a flute to dance. Usually he appears in the Mixed Kachina Dances or sometimes in a Night Dance. Despite these relatively minor appearances, he is thought of as a seducer of girls, a bringer of babies, a tutelary of hunting, and an excellent subject for the carving of tihus or kachina dolls. The artist has chosen to show this kachina in the relatively modest pose that he assumes in the Mixed Kachina Dance.

Monongya

The Lizard Kachina is one of the Fighting Kachinas, a group that furnishes individuals to chastise the clowns for their un-Hopi behavior. He is presumed to represent a particular species of lizard, the Crotophytus. This particular lizard is a brilliant turquoise color and very fast in movement.
Should a young man meet one, he would address it as his friend and ask for a favorable interview with his sweetheart, hoping that the lizard would help him. The kachina usually appears in the Mixed Kachina Dance but may also be seen in the Powamu. The illustration is of one of the fancier versions of this kachina. Many times they are quite plain in appearance.

110

Mongwa

The Great Horned Owl is best noted for his incessant war on the clowns. As the clowns follow their usual pattern of un-Hopi-like behaviour, a single silent figure will drift into one corner of the plaza and watch these uncouth fellows. When the clowns next appear, growing ever more boisterous in their actions, the Owl again appears and hoots solemnly. With each appearance he gets closer until he ends up talking with the clown chief who promptly blames all misbehaviour on the other clowns. But at the last performance, the Owl is joined by other Warrior Kachinas. They leap upon the clowns, douse them with water, beat them vigorously with willow switches or yucca blades, and leave them howling with remorse in a pile in the middle of the plaza. Here, the Owl appears as he disapprovingly watches the antics of the clowns. This is the personation that appears on Third Mesa.

Laqan

The Squirrel Kachina appears on all three mesas but has two rather distinct forms. The kachina shown in this illustration is very obviously a Second Mesa kachina with the feather ears. During the Kiva Dances in winter he is supposed to challenge any woman to take from him anything that she thinks worth having. However, he may appear also at Powamu or in the plaza dances in large numbers.

112

Toho

The Mountain Lion Kachina appears at Pachavu times as does the Tokoch (Wildcat) Kachina. When he carries yucca whips in his hand, he would be one of the Angry or Watching Kachinas. He may appear in the Mixed Kachina Dance with either Deer or Antelope Kachinas whom he leads for he is always in the front and is never caught. In this role he is a side dancer for the Deer or Antelope and carries a talavaiyi, a cane with eagle feathers and red horsehair fringe, in his hands. When he appears at Pachavu time on Second Mesa, he is one of the more important kachinas, but as pictured here he is simply the side dancer for the grazing animals.

Hon Kachina

The Bear Kachina is of such great strength that it is felt he can cure the sick. He appears in the kachina return or Soyal of First Mesa as the watchman or side dancer for the Chakwaina. In this role he appears a little different that he does in this illustration. He may come singly or in a group during the Palölökong Dance, and he may appear in a number of colors such as Sakwa Honau (Blue Bear) or as is illustrated — Kócha Honau (White Bear). Probably he is most familiar in the Mixed Kachina Dance, dancing outside the lines. His most distinctive features is the presence of a bear footprint on either cheek.

114

Honan Kachina

There are two types of Badger Kachinas: the old Hopi
Badger Kachina and a more recent import from the
Rio Grande. The old Hopi Badger was a curing kachina that
the Honani Clan brought from the ancient village of Kisiwu.
Prayers for the growth of healing herbs are given to him.
In recent years another type of Badger Kachina has made
his appearance, but it is not yet known whether this one
serves the same function or not. The Badger is illustrated
holding a gift that he will present to someone as he dances
in the Mixed Kachina Dance.

115

Wupá'ala

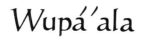

Very little is known of the Hopi Long-Horned Kachina except that he usually appears in the Mixed Kachina Dance. He seems to appear most frequently on First Mesa where he carries sheep scapulae in his right hand. Presumably he is patterned after the Zuni Sai-astasana as most Hopis will identify him as a Zuni Kachina. He appeared in the Bean Dance on Second Mesa a few years ago as a member of the procession carrying bow and arrows in the left hand and scapulae in the right.

Navuk'china

There are several varieties of Cactus Kachinas. Osök'china is the Chollo Cactus Kachina, already described. Navuk'china is the Prickly Pear Leaf Kachina and Yung'a Kachina, the Prickly Pear Fruit Kachina. Any of the Cactus Kachinas may appear as policemen or enforcer kachinas, and the staff that they carry often has a cactus joint attached at the end as a weapon. Despite the fancy appearance of this kachina he is an old Hopi personation. More often than not he wears two huzrunkwa, or warrior feathers, flat on the crown of the head which is painted in alternating black and white stripes. Over the right shoulder is thrown a buckskin cape that comes under the left arm and ties across the chest. The "flowers" on the cheeks are distinctly an innovation of the artist as they are usually a stylized circle or dot of red surrounded by a black band with white dots upon it.

Ai Kachina

The Ai (Rattle) Kachina is the same
kachina as the Aya (Colton No. 48). The only difference
is in the costume that is worn and the ceremony in
which the appearance takes place. In other words
this is the same kachina in two different aspects. The Ai
Kachina appears in the Mixed Kachina Dance in full
costume and the Aya as a runner. It is doubtful
that the Rattle Kachina ever carried the talavaiyi, the
staff that the artist has depicted in the left
hand of this kachina.

118

Tutumsi

Tutumsi is the Komanchi (Comanche)
Kachina. However, he most closely resembles the
Temtemsi of the Zuni which is not a Comanche Kachina.
Temtemsi, when he appears in Zuni, is spotted with
the blood of his victims, and many are the stories
relating to him. However, in Hopi he does not seem to be
a popular kachina, and there are very few dolls
made of him. He appears in the Mixed Dances but even
here his personations are few.

Hochani

Formerly Hochani was a much more popular
kachina than he is at present. He was probably introduced
to the Hopis from the Rio Grande Pueblos. In fact his
name is the Keresan term for Chief or Headman.
Legend has it that he was a Hopi who went to live in
the Rio Grande during adverse times and returned bringing
presents to the Hopi. He may appear in Kiva Dances
in the winter but most frequently is seen in the Mixed
Kachina Dances in the spring.

120

Sivu-i-quil Taka

The Pot Carrier Man is a
kachina of many names. When he appears as a runner, he
is generally called Matia, his costume is abbreviated
and no maiden accompanies him. If he appears with a
mana walking behind stirring the pot that he carries, he
is known by the name of Talakin. Other names
are Malachpeta and Malatsmo (Hand Kachina). Usually
the pot is carried by the strap being passed over the
forehead rather than the shoulders. The legs are either
painted or covered with white pants rather than with the
knitted stockings that are generally reserved for
the chief kachinas. In addition this is the only kachina
who wears wedding robe tassels for ears. The
tassels may be attached as earrings to the red ears or
simply hang alone from the side of the mask. The ruff is
of cloth, either gray or black and white as in the ruff
of the Zuni-derived kachinas.

121

Chospos-yaka-hentaka

The unprounceable name of this kachina may
be translated as the Turquoise Nose Plug Man or some
variation similar to this. He is also known as the Kipok
Kachina or the War Leader when he dresses in a
slightly different way. It is said that he was derived from
one of the Yuman tribes who formerly wore turquoise
nose ornaments. In addition his hair is pulled to the rear
and tied at the nape of the neck in the manner that
some of the Colorado River Indians dressed
their hair. He may appear with the Left-Handed Kachina,
also derived from the Western Indians, when the fight
with the clowns takes place in the plaza. If he does
not appear with the above kachina, he appears in
pairs. At this time he may either carry a whip or a handful
of arrows, using one of the arrows to prod the clowns.
He also appears in the Mixed Kachina Dance.

122

Tühavi

Tühavi is the Paralyzed Kachina, and legend has it that while he was paralyzed, he was carried by a friend who was blind. Together they were able to travel and hunt. Tühavi would tell his blind companion where to walk and how to aim his arrow when they needed food. Thus it is that when this kachina does appear he is usually carried by another kachina, most frequently the Mudhead. This kachina has apparently not been portrayed in a long time. He is shown in this illustration in an irregular position as he should be either seated with his legs spread flat on the ground or carried by some other kachina. The face does not have a white spot on either cheek, and the horizontal fan on the head is interspersed with red horsehair.

Tawa Kachina

The Sun Kachina is a representation of
the spirit of the Sun, though he may on occasion be
called the Sun Shield Kachina. He appears in a role
very similar to that of Nakiachop or Talavai, standing to
the side with a spruce tree in his left hand and a bell in
his right. Also, he may appear in a Mixed Dance
with the flute in his left hand that is associated with him in
many myths. He is not often personated.

124

Sohu Kachina

The Star Kachina is a strange
mixture with his fringed hunting shirt and kilt of
radiating turkey feathers. He does not resemble the usual
Hopi Kachina. He appears in the Mixed Kachina Dance
but never comes as a single kachina. Normally the
points of the stars have red stained "warrior" feathers on
the tips, and the top of the head is covered with
sheepskin dyed black, rather than real hair.

Navuk'china

Usually this kachina is called Pachok'china
but either name means the Cocklebur Kachina. He is
represented here as he appears in the Mixed Kachina Dance,
but he is more often seen as a runner. When he appears
as a runner, he does not carry the bow nor does he
wear any of the fancy gear around the waist. Instead
he wears a breechclout and carries a handful of
cockleburs which he blithely rubs into the hair of his
contestant if the latter fails to win the race. The
object that he holds in his right hand is supposed to be a
cocklebur plant. This plant grows in marshy places
when it rains and is thus a mimetic indicator for water.

Pautiwa

Pautiwa is the Zuni Sun God,
the most important of all Zuni Kachinas. But
among the Hopis he is simply one of many borrowed
kachinas that may be danced during the month of January
or appear in a Mixed Dance with many other Zuni
Kachinas. He has no function other than that of any
kachina — bringing rain and mist. In this version
the yellow line that usually surrounds the eyes has been
left out or deliberately made white. A rattle is placed
in the right hand instead of the two small crooked sticks
that he often carries, and the large clump of
plumes that normally appear on the rear of the head are
replaced with yellow parakeet feathers. Otherwise he
is a good representation.

Shulawitsi

This little Zuni Kachina is an almost
exact duplicate of the Hopi Kokosori and is most often
portrayed by a boy. Although he understands
all game, he does not usually carry a bow and arrow for
he is not a hunter. He may appear with game in hand or
hung over his shoulder. In another guise he may
come with cedar bark torch in hand. He may accompany
the other Zuni Kachinas in the Mixed Dance, but as
he is so close to Kokosori in appearance, it is sometimes
difficult to tell which kachina he is. He should not
have blue-ringed eyes, tube snout nor red ears. The bow and
quiver of arrows can be carried, but they are not usually.
He is shown here as he examines a
set of bear tracks.

Sipikne

This particular Zuni Kachina is often danced by the Hopis. His Zuni name is Salimopaiyakya but among the Hopis he may be called Sipikne or Talaimochovi. He dances in a very active manner bounding about and raising his knees much higher than the usual kachina. The dance is so demanding that only young men usually take this personation. He may appear in the Night Dances, the Bean Dance, a Mixed Dance, or in any other dance where it is felt that he would be appropriate. Sipikne may appear in several different colors but black or yellow seems to be the most favored. He very often functions as a guard to keep people back from certain other kachinas. Formerly bells were never used by this kachina, and part of the interest in his dance was that he danced so rapidly in complete silence. However, now he always wears sleigh bells.

Hakto

Hakto is a kachina that was introduced from the
Zuni sometime in the last 100 years. In Zuni he is known
as Yamuhakto and he always accompanies the Salako;
among the Hopis he appears only with the Sio Salako and
has had his name abbreviated to Hakto. The Zuni
name refers to "carrying wood on his head." The
marks of color on each temple are referred to as
perspiration marks.

Sai-astasana

Sai-astasana is the Zuni Rain Priest of the North who accompanies the Salako when they appear at Zuni. At Hopi he usually appears with other Zuni kachinas such as Shulawitsi, Pautiwa, Sipikne, and Hakto in a Mixed Dance. The kachina carries a cluster of scapulae in his right hand and a sack of meal in his left hand with a bow. Usually the yellow feathers on the crown of the head are attached to a paho.

Chiwap

Chiwavi means "blowing sand," hence the name of this kachina is Blowing Sand, or more properly, the Coarse Blowing Sand Kachina. The name is shortened to Sand Kachina. This kachina does not appear very often; when he does appear he is masked on First and Second Mesa but not on Third Mesa. He tells stories and criticizes like an uncle when he appears in the Soyohim Kachina Dances. This may be a recent Third Mesa masked appearance, but if so, it is unknown to the majority of Hopis who have seen it.

Payik'ala

Listed in Colton (1959:59) as Pahi-ala, the name
properly should be Payik'ala, the Three-Horned Kachina.
Colton also states that he was introduced from Zuni
to First Mesa in 1921; however, other Hopis remember
dancing this kachina on Third Mesa before the founding of
Hotevilla in 1906. This is a good illustration of the
kachina as he appears in the Mixed Dance.

Piokak

This kachina dances in the kivas but otherwise little is known of his function. He may appear on all three mesas during the Night Dances in March. His name refers to the sound of clapping or foot slapping. The general appearance of this kachina is reminiscent of the Rio Grande kachinas although he has appeared among the Hopis for more than seventy-five years.

134

Hututu

Hututu takes his name from the cry that he makes. The name is the same in Zuni where this kachina comes from. He appears with many of the other Zuni kachinas when they dance at Hopi. These Zuni kachinas are Hopi-made and personated and there is almost no attempt to Hopi-ize them. Probably the only difference that may be noted by the observer at a dance where both Hututu and Sai-astasana appear is the prescence of a horn on Sai-astasana's head.

Samo'a Wutaka

Broad-leaf Yucca Old Man appears most frequently
in the Bean Dance at Hano. He represents the spirit of all
the sweet fruit of the cactus such as the agave, the
broad and narrow-leaf yucca, etc. His mask is covered
with the juice of these plants. He is presumed to know
many songs that will compel the Clouds to come and bring
rain for the crops. Samo'a Wutaka very often appears with
the clowns during the Mixed Dances in the spring.
His costume is usually old and shabby clothing of any type,
as the mask is the only important aspect. He is shown
here bearing narrow-leaf yucca, but he could just
as well carry cactus fruit. However, his hair is nearly
always gray or white for he is an old man.

136

Loi´isa

Presumably this kachina is the only one that the Tewa brought with them from the Rio Grande, though it may be one that was brought from Acoma. He appears with the Mixed Kachinas singing to the Clouds to hasten the rain. He appeals only to the Clouds of the North and West. He usually appears in slovenly shabby clothes with a rattle in his right hand and a bunch of willow in his left.

Pöökang Kwivi Kachina

The Proud War God Kachina represents the spirit
of Pöökanghoya as he would appear in his best finery.
There seem to be several types of Pöökang Kachinas, this
being simply the dressiest one. He often appears in the
Mixed Kachina Dances but may also appear in evening
dances in the kivas. He is one of the so-called Fighting
Kachinas. The statement in Colton (Colton:1959:62) that
this kachina has "warrior tracks" on his chest did not
refer to bare feet. It refers to the double lines that are
apparent on the kachina's arms — these are puukongkuku
or warrior tracks.

138

Kawai-i Kachina

The Horse Kachina derives its name from the
Spanish word for horse — *caballo*. Oddly enough this
is not an old kachina and was probably introduced
less than ninety years ago. But it still carries a Spanish
name. He may usually be seen during the Soyohim or
Mixed Kachina Dances but may also appear in the Bean
Dance Parade, or in groups on Third Mesa and sometimes
in the kiva dances. He is far less popular today than
he was a few years ago.

Muzribi

The Bean Kachina is one of the so-called Rugan
Kachinas in that he is frequently accompanied by a Mana
who rasps for him. When he is accompanied by a Mana
he appears in the regular kachina dances. If he appears
in the Mixed Kachina Dances he usually is unescorted. His
purpose is inherent in his name; he helps the Beans to
grow. His color may vary somewhat but this painting
shows his most common appearance.

140

Hapota

Hapota is a drummer who is masked. He may appear with any group that needs a single drummer, but there are many other kachinas who can be chosen for this role as well. Like these other drummers he may be coerced into helping the clowns in some particular prank or be the butt of the clown's humor, particularly during the Mixed Kachina Dances. Hapota is usually rather active and moves with the dancers.

Hishab Kachina

This particular kachina has disappeared from the Hopi pantheon and is perpetuated only through publications. The Hopis do not know how he danced nor what his purpose was, although his name indicates that he is a Mormon Tea (Ephedra) Kachina.

Pash Kachina

The Pash or Field Kachina appears on all three mesas. He comes with the clowns and acts like one of them. He appears to be closer to the Piptuka than he is to a kachina in his actions, nevertheless the Hopis consider him to be a kachina. He is most often seen in the Mixed Kachina Dances. He is portrayed here as described by Colton, but earlier examples indicate that he formerly appeared in a breechclout and with a maiden shawl over one shoulder as his sole garments.

Wukoqala

Wukoqala, the Big Forehead Kachina, is an old kachina
on Third Mesa. He formerly appeared in the Mixed Kachina
Dances and urged the boys of the village to be good
hunters. This is the reason that he carries a rabbit stick
in his left hand during the dance. However, this dance has
not been given in a long time. The last one was
probably held in 1926.

144

. YOCHI **Yoche**

The Apache Kachina is a comic figure or caricature
that may appear during the Kiva Dances both early and
late, or with the Soyohim later in the year. A group
of them frequently will appear in the Buffalo Dances during
the Kachina season. Their actions are usually those
that one would expect of Apaches on the warpath. They
are often used in conjunction with the clowns. This
particular personage is a mixture of the more recent type
of Supai Kachina and the Zuni version of an Apache.
Since this is one of the lesser kachinas, it makes little
difference how he dresses as long as the appearance is that
of an Apache. The posture for removing an arrow
from the quiver is incorrect.

Yung'a

It is said that the name of this kachina is derived from the Spanish word for prickly pear, *tuna*. However there is just as much reason to believe that this word, *yung'a*, is an old Hopi word. As a kachina he appeared just prior to the turn of the century and was personated only a few times on First Mesa. He has been perpetuated more through the use of dolls rather than in dances. His function on Third Mesa was to insure the cleaning of springs, but on First Mesa he seems to have appeared primarily in the Soyohim. The illustration is essentially the way that he appears except for the yucca held in the right hand. This is usually a stick with a pad of cactus attached to the end.

146

Yung'a Mana

When Yung'a appears in the Soyohim he is accompanied by the Yung'a Mana. Yung'a Mana usually carries a basket with pads of prickly pear in it. In her left hand she carries a set of wooden tongs that she uses to handle the cactus pads. She is dressed in the manner of the Hano Kachin Mana. The tongs in the left hand are incorrectly drawn for they are not just two sticks; they should be attached at one end.

Paski Kachina

The Field House Kachina is presumably a planting kachina for when he appears he carries a hoe. He is sometimes known as the Hoe Kachina or as the Pashtabi Kachina. His appearance is for success in the fields.

148

Tiwenu

Tiwenu is an import from the Rio Grande, but it is nearly impossible to tell which village he came from. He is called Santo Domingo, Laguna, or Acoma with equal impartiality. However he arrived, he dances in the manner of a social dance. Normally the mask has a little more decoration than is present on this one, and the chin is nearly always all black.

Umtoinaqa

Umtoinaqa is the Shooting Thunder Kachina. He acts
as a policeman or guard during the Bean Dance but is
most commonly seen in the Mixed Kachina Dances. The
bull roarer that he carries in his hand is used to
imitate the sound of thunder. Usually this kachina does
not have the double colored eyes. He wears a huzrunkwa,
or warrior feather, on the crown of the head and a double
warrior's bandolier over the chest; a bow is carried
in the left hand.

Tasap Kachina

This kachina was apparently inspired by one of the Navajo Gods, Naastadji, the Fringe-mouth God. However, he has no Hopi name other than Tasap or Navajo Kachina. This Tasap is not seen too often, but when he does appear it is usually in the Soyohim. This illustration in no way resembles the same kachina that appears in Fewkes (1903:Pl.XXXV), but it is the same personage. The illustration is a Third Mesa form.

Tawa Koyung Kachina

The Tawa Koyung Kachina represents the Peacock or
Sun Turkey. The name reflects the Hopis' thought of their
first impression of a peacock. He is not a common kachina
and appears most often in the Soyohim. Apparently
he was inspired from the Rio Grande pueblos and spread
to Hopi country before the turn of the century.
Usually the body is painted with alternating yellow and
blue shoulders, forearms, and calves, in order that the
kachina be more colorful.

Homahtoi Kachina

Homahtoi is supposed to be a Zuni name, and he is presumed to have been introduced to the Hopis from that pueblo. He is one of the many Ichiwo or Angry Kachinas. He is not a common kachina but may be seen from time to time with the Mixed Kachinas. There are many variations in the painting of the mask with regard to the individual elements, but the general form is always that which appears in this illustration.

Fox Kachina

Letaiyo or Fox Kachina may appear in the Soyohim dances, but usually he is personated as a runner. As a runner, he dresses very simply in order that he may run more rapidly. As a Soyohim dancer he appears as a single figure in line with the other kachinas. Usually there is a track with only three toes on the cheeks of this kachina. He is portrayed here as he would appear in the Mixed Kachina Dance.

Mahu

Mahu is the Cicada Kachina that appears in the
Night or Kiva Dances early in the year or during the
Soyohim of late spring. Presumably he appears as a prayer
for the arrival of summer when the real cicada appears.
With the exception of the black and white rings about
the calves and forearms, this is the way the
kachina usually appears.

155

I'she

There appear to be two varieties of I'she, the Mustard Green Kachina. One type has elongated eyes like the Squirrel Kachina and wears a ring of eagle feathers on top of the head. The second variety is closest to the one portrayed by Bahnimptewa. Both represent the Mustard Green and its appearance in early spring as a wild food. Customarily the head of this kachina is divided by a vertical band of red between the eyes that joins a band of red placed horizontally *above* the eyes. The field to the right of this division is blue and to the left, yellow.

156

Sotungtaka

This kachina has appeared rather recently on the Hopi mesas, probably within the last twenty years. He usually appears as a side dancer with a group of corn dancers or Avachhoya. It is said that he comes from Santo Domingo and is the uncle of the corn dancers. He moves with very graceful motions gesturing with the objects that he carries in his hands.

Angwusi

Angwus Kachina is the Crow Kachina. This Kachina
is one of the warriors who make war on the clowns during
the Plaza Dances or who appear in the Soyohim of late
spring. He comes to threaten the clowns for their
immoderate behavior, appearing again and again until
finally he and others who have the same function descend
upon the clowns and thoroughly chastize them. Here
he carries the whips butt first, and is probably
appearing to warn the clowns.

Heoto

Heoto appears in the Kiva Dances, Soyohim, and Plaza Dances. He is a variant or related form of the Chakwaina and appears in a very similar role. He also functions as a guard during the Powamu.

Heoto Mana

Heoto Mana dances on all three mesas. Her function is very similar to that of Hé-é-e, the Warrior Maiden. In this role she acts as a guard during the Pachavu procession. She also appears in all of the performances that Heoto does.

Kuwan Heheya

The Kuwan Heheya or "Colorful" Heheya is one of the group dancers often chosen for the Niman Kachina on First Mesa. They are accompanied by Kachin Manas who dance in a separate line, kneel and rasp at certain parts of the ceremony. Again, the ceremony is to bring rain for the partly matured crops, and they are asked, as the Hemis Kachina is asked, to tell the supernaturals to bring rain. The Kuwan Heheya are usually accompanied by two side dancers: one is the Heheya's Uncle and the other is the Heheya Youth.

Turtle Kachina

This particular version of the Kahaila Kachina is the Turtle Kachina of Second Mesa. There are several others that are called Kahaila, and each of these has an additional name, making it very easy to be confused. The Turtle dance is believed to have been given first at Shipaulovi as a line dance and to have come from Acoma sometime before the turn of the century. He is still most often seen in Shipaulovi as a line dancer. He is not an especially attractive kachina, but he has nice songs.

Pawik

The Hopi Duck Kachina used to be danced with much greater frequency than it has been in recent years. The kachina is a prayer for rain or moisture, and as such he appears in the Mixed Kachina Dances and the Kiva Dances much earlier in the year as well as later in the Plaza Dances. He is very often danced in June when there is great need for water. There are three kinds of Ducks that may appear in the dances: the most common is the Hopi Duck shown in this illustration; second, a Zuni Duck that is rather rare; and also a form of Wuyaköte that has lost its identity with time. The illustration shows the Duck as he offers a gift of roast corn to someone in the audience. However the staff that he carries in his left hand does not have the customary greenery. It should be a full staff of unpeeled willow with the leaves left on top of the stem.

Kweo Kachina

Whenever the Deer or Antelope Kachinas dance in the plaza, another kachina is very frequently seen with them — the Wolf Kachina (Kweo). He is their side dancer, and the stick he holds in his hands is said to represent trees and bushes that he hides behind as he watches them. When he appears, the Deer and the Antelope are wary because in real life he is the hunter of antelope. After the dance it is customary for the Hopis to offer the Wolf Kachina cornmeal or prayer feathers so that he will use his knowledge to find and capture these game animals. For some reason this kachina calls forth the Hopi urge to elaborate. He is not usually this colorful nor realistic and is consequently more forceful in appearance.

164

Antelope Kachina

Like most of the game animals, the Antelope is danced as a prayer for the increase of his kind. When he appears, whether in the kiva or as a group in the plaza, it is in the hope that more of his kind will be around for harvesting by the Hopis. The Hopis may offer him cornmeal and prayer feathers and explicitly state the wish that he will remain and allow them to take some members of the Antelope family. The stick that he holds in his hands represents the front legs of the animal when he walks or dances. The horns of this kachina are incorrect, as they are placed backward, and it is difficult to recognize what the artist intended them to be. However, the remainder of the kachina is well done.

165

Deer Kachina

One of the very popular Plaza Kachina Dances is that of the Deer Kachina. He has power over the rain, and of course, when he dances, he is a prayer for increase of deer. Usually when a group of these dancers appear they are accompanied by a Wolf or Mountain Lion Kachina as a side dancer. Presumably the first Deer Kachinas were brought from Awatovi, which may be correct as they retain a strong Rio Grande appearance. The position that this kachina usually assumes when he dances is that of bending forward at the waist and resting the front part of the body upon the short stick that is carried in his hands.

166

Cow Kachina

The Cow or Wakas Kachina is a recent introduction into the Hopi area; he seems to have reached First Mesa around the turn of the century and was introduced by a Hano man. By 1911 he was being personated on Third Mesa, and in recent years he has been a favorite at Moenkopi. It is rather strange that this kachina took so long to be introduced to the Hopis and that, when he was, he should carry a Spanish name — for Wakas is obviously derived from the Spanish *vaca*. Many times at the end of its appearance in an ordinary kachina dance, the spectators will take the juniper or feathers from this kachina to put into their houses and corrals in hope that their stock will increase. This is a poor picture of the Cow Kachina.

Hólolo

Hólolo appears in two distinct varieties. The face of one has varicolored crescents under the eyes and many times is referred to as the Moon Kachina, Muyaow. The other has large ears, and the decoration that appears on these ears runs on to the face as well. It is sometimes called Wupa Nakava Kachina or Big Ears. The generic name of Hólolo comes from the sound of the song that he sings. Third Mesa Hopis maintain that they originated this kachina, and that it was then borrowed by the other mesas. These two kachinas appear most often in the Plaza Dance but may also be seen in the Mixed Dance or in the Kiva Dances. It is said that this kachina speeds the birth of a child.

168

Ho'óte

Ho'óte is an extremely popular kachina because of his well-liked songs. He appears as a group in the ordinary kachina dances and sometimes in the Niman. The symbols between his eyes and on his forehead are said to be those of flowers, and therefore his dance forecasts the flowers of spring. It is unfortunate that this kachina's name, Ho'óte and Colton's No. 105 (A'hote) are so close in pronunciation. Colton calls No. 104 Aho'ote or Ho'óte, and his name for No. 105 is A'hote. I have chosen to identify Colton's No. 104 as Ho'óte and No. 105 as A'hote in hope of reducing confusion. However the confusion of names appears to be in the realm of linguistics rather than in the minds of the Hopis. This kachina may appear with a buckskin kilt and silver belt coupled with the presence of the yellow triangle on the face. When the kachina wears the embroidered robe he should have a blue triangle between his eyes.

A'hote

A'hote may appear in any of the directional colors but
the two most common colors are the yellow A'hote
(Sikyahote) or the blue (Sakwahote). In a Plaza Dance it
is not unusual to see a line of Sakwahote with several
Sikyahote, and a white or red form as well. All indications
in his costume point to inspiration from a Plains-type
warrior, particularly the feather headdress. A'hote may
appear in the Mixed Kachina Dances, or the Palölökong
Dances and the Plaza Dance. In his left hand he very
frequently carries roast or boiled corn that is given out to
the audience during his performance. The artist has
shown Sakwahote as the subject of this illustration.

Avachhoya

Avachhoya or Qá-ö is the Spotted Corn Kachina who appears in the Pamuya and in the regular kachina dances. Generally this Corn Kachina dances with such a lively step that only the boys or young men will take the part. They do not sing and are always accompanied by a drummer and chorus, usually Koyemsi. Sometimes two of these kachinas will dance on the plaza by the side of the Niman Kachinas. Holding nothing in their hands, they make motions and signs describing such figures as clouds or cornstalks or whatever is being sung about at the time. Probably no other kachina name has quite so many different forms grouped together. It is apparently a generic term, at least nowadays, that covers a multitude of dancers whose function is to aid in the production of corn. The old Hopi style of Avachhoya was a figure with rings painted upon the body and face and four crossed feathers upon the head. This is probably the closest approach to the written descriptions of Avachhoya, and yet it is just as close to the Laguna Swaying Man. It is a hybrid figure that any Hopi will call Avachhoya — one of the Corn Dancers.

Angak'china

The Long-haired Kachina is one of the most pervasive
of all kachinas. It is danced from the Rio Grande to the Hopi
Mesas in almost the same form. Among the Hopis
there are many varieties but the regular Angak'china is
the one portrayed here. They appear in a group and sing a
very melodious song which may be one of the reasons
that they are such favorites. They are often used for
the Niman Kachina on First Mesa coming with the Köcha
Mana. In fact they have danced in late August on First
Mesa in direct contradiction to the feeling that only
Masau'u can be danced out of season. Probably this was
due to the presence of the Tewa people who do not have a
closed kachina season. Their purpose is to bring rain,
and it is said that they seldom dance without the appearance
of a soft gentle rain to help the crops grow. The
Angak'china shown in this illustration is the variety known
as Hokyan Angak'china, so named because of the
peculiar step that he uses in dancing. He is also called
the Red-bearded Angak'china. His function is exactly the
same as the regular Angak'china — to bring rain for
the crops. Angak'china is shown in this illustration as he
delivers presents in mid-summer.

Katoch Angak'china

The Katoch Angak'china is the Barefooted, Long-haired Kachina, and he dances in the same manner as the other Angak'china. They may appear in the kivas or as groups in the plaza but never in the Mixed Kachina Dances. There are several variations of the standard Angak'china, of which this is but one, and they all follow a common song pattern. The songs of this Angak'china are the same as the regular version except for the beginnings. Köcha Mana usually accompanies the Katoch Angak'china as do several Chukuwimkia or clowns. Normally this kachina does not wear turkey feathers across the beard or a macaw feather up the back of the head. In addition the body should be marked with yellow bars on arms and chest, or an intaglio double line that goes up the arm, across the shoulder and down the chest. Despite this and the tiny feet, it is a good portrayal of the kachina.

Angak'chin Mana

Called either the Angak'chin Mana or the Köcha
Mana (White Girl), this personage always accompanies
the Angak'china when he appears and dances in the
plaza. There are usually about half or a third as many
Manas as there are kachinas, and they dance in a separate
line, gesturing with the spruce boughs that they hold in
each hand. At times they will carry gourd, notched
stick and scapulae; then they kneel and rasp at set intervals
during the dance. There are many Zuni characteristics
present in this figure, from the way the hair is dressed to
the footless stockings on the legs. Possibly Zuni is her
original home. The hands and feet of this Mana
should be painted yellow.

174

Takursh Mana

Yellow Corn Maiden appears with a variety of kachinas, Angak'china, Ma'alo, Pawik and others. She may sometimes be seen with the Köcha Mana. They dance in a line separate from the other kachinas but following the same pattern of dance, turning as the others do, gesturing as they do. Their only deviation is when they kneel and place large gourds on the ground to rasp. Takursh Mana is shown here as she kneels to rasp. In her right hand is a sheep scapulae and in her left a notched stick, while in front of her is a large painted gourd that has been cleaned and hardened. The lower edge of the gourd is padded around the opening. The stick is placed across the gourd, and the scapula is pulled up and down over the stick. The gourd forms a resonating chamber, and the tone is varied by the direction of stroke and the speed.

175

Ma'alo Kachina

Around the turn of the century this was one of the most popular kachinas. He was danced as a Niman Kachina along with Hemis, Angak'china and Kuwan Heheya on First Mesa and he appeared in regular kachina dances on the other two mesas. In time his popularity seems to have faded, and he does not dance as often nowadays. He usually appears with Takursh Mana as his sister, dancing in a separate line alongside of him. He is sometimes referred to as the Stick Kachina because of the staff he carries in his left hand. The staff is not the usual type carried by this kachina but is more like that carried by Pawik'china. Usually the forehead band of this kachina is white with black dots rather than the reverse.

176

Tunei-nili

Tunei-nili is a Navajo-derived kachina. He is the individual who looks after the Navajo or Tasap Kachinas and is usually called a side dancer for them. However, he may not always appear with the Tasap. He was inspired by the Navajo Rain Gods, the Tone-nili, who appear on the sixth day of the Navajo Yeibichai Ceremony. The name Tunei-nili Bitzai means "little wash" or "little river grandfather." He sometimes appears with the Velvet Shirt Kachinas also. The face is somewhat elaborated, but otherwise this is a good portrayal of this kachina.

Kau-a Kachina

Kau-a or Quoi-a Kachina is the old-style Navajo Kachina who sings in Navajo when he appears in a regular kachina dance. There are two quite distinct types of this kachina; the older style has a yellow and red chevron over the nose, and both ears are enormous tufts of yarn and feathers. He may appear in Plaza Dances or in the Pachavu at Mishongnovi. He may also appear in the line of the Chief Kachinas where he serves as a helper for the Pachavu Manas. The second type has not been illustrated by Bahnimptewa. The name is derived from the sound that the kachina makes as he dances, a coughing "kowa" or "kow-ah." He is also called a Navajo or Tasap Kachina, and lastly and very undiplomatically he is called Sisiyak or Runny Nose. As Kau-a or Quoi-a he is correct in all details.

178

Kau-a Kachin Mana

This is a very distinctive Kachin Mana for there is no other quite like it. The closest is the Hano Mana who lacks the peculiar Navajo snout and hairdress of this mana. She accompanies the Kau-a Kachina and like her brother is a Navajo Kachina. During the dance she carries a basket. In some cases she kneels and uses the rasper and scapula on the basket while Kau-a stands in line in front of her. She never accompanies the Mongakwi Kau-a. As she kneels to rasp in this illustration the two turkey feathers, the unusual snout and the hairdress are clearly shown.

Tasap Kachina

It has been incorrectly stated that the Tasap Kachina came from the Navajo. It does *only* in the sense that the Bee Kachina comes from bees. It was never a Navajo dance figure. But it is instead the Hopis' interpretation of their neighbors. He is a very popular kachina. This popularity is the reason for the variety of Tasap Kachinas and is undoubtedly one of the reasons that he may be selected for the Niman Ceremony instead of the Hemis Kachina. Usually he performs in the plaza as a regular kachina dance. The actual dance is one of rather monotonous stamping that is broken at intervals by some rather interesting turns and calls. This is by far the most common form of the Tasap Kachina.

180

Tasap Kachin Mana

The Navajo Maiden dances alongside the Tasap Kachina in the regular kachina dance, but she may also appear at odd intervals during the kachina season. The mask of the Tasap Mana is a Hopi caricature of the Navajo and their manner of gesturing with the lower lip. Despite this she is part of a group that is very popular with the Hopis. Tasap Mana is shown in this illustration in a fancier version than she often appears. In recent years ribbons have been added to the costume of this Mana while before she was quite plain.

Tasap Yeibichai

The Grandfather of the Navajo Kachina is one of the more enjoyable features of the Navajo Kachina Dance. He does not speak but pantomimes whatever he wants. He starts the dance, acting as a leader in both singing and dancing. His dance step is an exaggeration, and a very lively one, that may be interspersed with a comic action such as the request for food — mountains of food. All of these requests are done in pantomimes that bring laughter to the audience. The Grandfather or Uncle has several variations but the one portrayed here is the one that is most often seen. Because he is shown in profile the cornstalk painted down the center of the face does not show clearly. However the corn ears at the side and rear of the face are clearly visible. The buckskin cape over the shoulders is usually very long, almost brushing the ground, and is used with great dramatic effect.

Tuma-uyi

Tuma-uyi (Tuma-öi) is one of the very old kachinas of the Hopis. He has not been performed in recent years, but when he did appear, he came in a group, or in the Powamu Ceremony. However he can be impersonated at any time. His name means "white chin" and seems to derive from the white clay that is used to coat kachina dolls before they are painted. Other than the primary function of all kachinas — to bring rain — the purpose of this kachina is unknown.

183

Konin Kachina

The Konin or Supai Kachina appears in a regular kachina dance and is a representation of the Hopis' neighbors to the west, the Havasupai Indians. There are several varieties of this kachina, and the male kachina that is illustrated is the one that in recent years has come more into vogue. He usually appears with a chorus of singers and a "sister" or Konin Mana. This is the male kachina in a characteristic dance pose. Most dolls are not made like this version of the Konin Kachina.

Kahaila

This kachina is presumed to be from the Rio Grande as his name is Keresan. Fewkes shows a good drawing of this kachina in Pl. XLVII of his publication *Hopi Kachinas* but calls the personation "Kwacus Alek Taka." This name simply means "eagle feathers erect man," a descriptive term for Kahaila. The kachina appears in a regular kachina dance with Alo Mana and is often called the Hunter Kachina. This is a Rio Grande-derived kachina, and it should be wearing the white and black boots with the skunk tail anklets rather than the Hopi moccasins.

Sio Salako

The Sio Salako is a Hopi interpretation of the Shalako
Ceremony of Zuni and thus receives the name Sio (Zuni).
Sio Salako is portrayed like neither the Zuni nor the
Hopi Salako, but is instead a separate entity. He was
introduced to the Hopis by a Tewa man around 1850 and
first appeared as a group of four kachinas. Since that
time changes in ceremonial have reduced the number to one
and added Salako Mana that formerly did not appear. He
appears in the late spring on very rare occasions and is
thought to be especially efficacious in bringing rain.
A view of this nine-foot kachina is a rare sight indeed.
Usually for this kachina the feathers all turn toward the
body with the exception of the bottom row. They are
reversed and consequently flare outward, giving the base of
the figure the appearance of wearing a petticoat.

Sio Salako Mana

Sio Salako Mana accompanies the Sio Salako in appearances at Hopi, (one visit is recorded at Second Mesa in 1924) but she is not an import from Zuni, despite her name. Normally when this Mana appears, she wears a maiden shawl rather than the embroidered wedding robe.

Kwivi Kachina

Kwivi is actually a term that means someone who is overly dressed or too proud of his appearance, sporty. It can be used for any kachina who wears lots of silver and is very fancy. However, in this case it has become the name for a type of Navajo Kachina. Usually he appears in a regular kachina dance and may be seen on all three mesas. He is said to have been a Zuni type that was introduced at Mishongnovi in 1899, but he has very little about him that points to a Zuni origin. He is depicted here in the Third Mesa style.

188

Sio Avachhoya

Frequently Sio Avachhoya is called Nawisa, as is Sipikne. This term, Nawisa, seems to be a class rather than a specific name among the Hopis. However, the name Sio Avachhoya means Zuni Corn Dancer and he is made and danced as a Hopi kachina, although he may have been introduced from Zuni a long time ago. He is usually seen in the Plaza Dances of late spring, although he does sometimes appear in Pamuya at First Mesa. His function is the same as that of the ordinary Avachhoya. The manner in which this kachina is dressed indicates that he may have originated even farther east than Zuni.

189

Marao Kachina

This kachina may derive his name from the fact that
the headdress he wears is the same as the one appearing on
the Mamzrau, the participants in an important women's
ceremony. Despite the name, the kachina is dressed in
a style much closer to that of the Navajo Kachinas
than anyone else. He appears in Plaza Dances in late spring.
There are several varieties of this kachina present on the
mesas, but there does not seem to be any variation in
naming. This illustration shows the tripod headdress that
is found on both this kachina and the performer
in the Mamzrau.

190

Navan Kachina

The Navan or Velvet Shirt Kachina is a comparatively recent kachina as it seems to have originated in Moenkopi sometime after 1900. He is one of the more colorful kachinas in a regular kachina dance with his bright ribbons and flowers. He may also appear in Kiva Dances. This is a very good illustration of this kachina.

Movitkuntaka

Many times new kachinas are brought out to join their
peers. Usually this occurs when someone dreams of a
kachina, and it appears in a different form. The Hopi
men will then compose songs, clarify its appearance and
present it at a dance. The Yucca Skirt Kachina is an
example of this process even though he is not completely
new as he was preceded by the Yucca Skirt Hu Kachina.
Movitkuntaka is noted for another thing in Hopi minds:
that is whenever he has been performed, unseasonably cold
weather has followed immediately with disastrous
results for the crops. As a result, Movitkuntaka does not
appear anymore. The illustration shows the strong
similarities that exist between this kachina and Marau as
well as the Yucca Skirt Hu Kachina.

192

Kyash Kachina

There is apparently a complete break in the history of the Parrot Kachina. His appearance on First Mesa before the turn of the century is quite different from his appearance eighty years later on Second Mesa. Between these two personations no dolls were made that were recognizable as the Parrot Kachina, nor were any dances given as the paraphernalia was not available. In 1965 a Parrot Dance was given as a regular dance for the first time in several generations. Formerly it had been given in the Water Serpent Ceremony on First Mesa. This kachina's purpose seems to be one of bringing summer growth plus the increase of parrots. This is the appearance of the Second Mesa Parrot Kachina.

Hano Mana

Hano Mana appears with the variety of Long-haired
Kachinas known as the Hokyang and as such may be called
Hokyang Mana. Since this dance was derived from the
eastern pueblos she may also be called Hopok Mana. She
is most often found in regular kachina dances
accompanying the line dancers as a rasper or "sister";
however, she may appear in Kiva Dances as well. Normally
she does not carry anything in her hands and dances
with many gestures to illustrate the context of the songs
that are sung. It is difficult to tell which form is pictured
here as she almost never carries anything in her hands.

194

Kawaika'a Kachina

As his name implies, this kachina comes from Laguna. He was borrowed from the Laguna by the Zuni. There a visiting Hopi man saw the dance and liked it, took time to learn the songs, and brought the kachina to First Mesa. In regular performances he dances in rows like the Third Mesa Poli Kachina. In addition he may appear as a Distributing or Talavai Kachina in the Powamu, as an Uncle with the Long-haired Kachina, or in the Soyohim. This kachina is shown essentially the way that he would be seen in the Soyohim.

Alo Mana

There seems little doubt that this Kachin Mana is
the same as Köcha Mana that accompanies the Angak'china.
The only difference is what each carries in its hands. Alo
Mana in this illustration wears a horsehair beard. In
the illustration of Köcha Mana she wears a feather beard,
but this is not a distinctive difference.

196

Ka'e

Ka'e is one of the many Corn Dancers. The Corn Dancers are probably the most popular of all the kachinas, and because of this popularity, they can appear in the Kiva Dances, Plaza Dances, and Mixed Dances. Whenever Ka'e or another of the Corn Dancers appears, he represents a prayer for the fruition and growth of corn. The costume worn here is similar in style to that of Rio Grande Corn Kachinas.

Palölökong Kachina

The Water Serpent Kachina is seen most often in the Soyohim or Plaza Dances but has also appeared in other ceremonies such as the Bean Dance Parade. Fewkes (1903:84) reports this kachina dancing with the Snow Kachina at the reopening of a spring on First Mesa. Palölökong Kachina is not a common personation. He is not often made as a doll, probably because he is believed to cause swollen stomachs. This appearance portrays him during a Mixed Kachina Dance.

Na-uikuitaka

Peeping Out Man is so named because it is felt that his eyes are peeping out over the top of the lower part of the mask. He is a fairly common dancer, who appears in the Mixed Kachina Dances, in regular Plaza Dances, and at times in the Night Dances in March. He is derived from the Santo Domingo Harvest Dancers.

Möna Kachina

The River or Thunder Kachina appears singly in the Mixed Kachina Dances. His function seems to be simply that of encouraging the flow of water. He appears most often on Third Mesa, and there is a possibility that he may be limited to that mesa.

Corn Dancer

This Corn Dancer is one of the Rugan Kachinas (Rasping Kachinas). They are accompanied by Manas who use gourd scapulae and rasps as musical instruments to accompany the kachinas during their dance. This kachina appears in a regular dance during the spring and is danced to promote the growth of corn. This is a good portrayal of this kachina.

Nayaiyataka

Nayaiyataka is a fairly recent import from the Rio Grande area, and he still retains the appearance of the Rio Grande Kachinas. He appears in the Plaza Dances, and his function seems to be that of the Avachhoya — the production of corn or the aid in its growth.

Harvester Kachina

The Harvester Kachina is simply another of the many Corn Dancers that appear in the late spring in regular kachina dances. Their function is to promote the growth of the corn crop. Colton calls this variety Rugan C as he is accompanied by a Mana that rasps.

Kuwantotim

The Kuwantotim is not a dancing kachina. He is rather a masked singer that appears with the kachinas. Many times when the kachinas appear, they must have a drummer or a chorus of singers with them. When the chorus appears, the members also wear masks which are usually very simple in construction and design. Painted here, the Kuwantotim carries a drum, as does Hapota, but probably only one of the Kuwantotim would carry the drum, and the others in the chorus would not.

Nihiyo

Nihiyo is a fancy version of the Navajo Kwivi-style of kachina. He appears in the Mixed Kachina Dance in the spring and is really a favorite kachina. Therefore he may also appear in a regular dance at any time in the Plaza. This kachina is presumed by all Hopis to have come from the Navajo, probably inspired by one of their dances. This is a good illustration of the Nihiyo Kachina.

Poli Sio Hemis Kachina

It is a little difficult to understand how this kachina
came by his complicated name. He is the Zuni Jemez
Butterfly Kachina. He is a fairly close relative of
the Third Mesa Poli Kachina and is probably an adaption
of a Rio Grande Kachina. He usually dances in the
ordinary Plaza Dance.

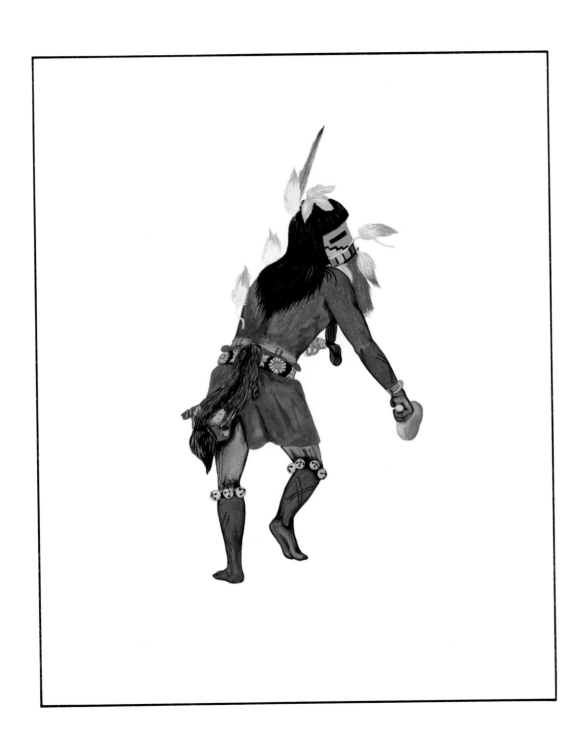

Tasap Angak'china

This variety of the Angak'china appears occasionally, but he is not common today. Most Hopis do not recognize him as the Navajo Long-haired Kachina. He dances in the typical Long-haired Kachina fashion, differing from him only in the appearance of the mask and in the fact that he wears a red kilt. He should be considered a variety of the Angak'china. Normally this kachina appears in moccasins rather than barefooted. In his earlier appearances he did not wear bells about the knees nor have the fancier feathers on his head. These are innovations that have appeared recently. The body is nearly always white, with yellow shoulders.

Sikyachantaka

Sikyachantaka is an old Hopi Kachina. It is said that
a long time ago when the Hopis were having a famine and
the Spanish had driven off their sheep, they decided to
have a kachina dance. At that time Sikyachantaka did not
have a name but one man in the village had a cow, and
he killed the animal and fed these kachinas the entrails of
the cow. Hence their name, "holding entrails in the
mouth." They dance in a similar manner to the Tasap
Kachina during regular kachina dances in the plaza. This
illustration shows the most common
form of Sikyachantaka.

Tuskiapaya

The Crazy Rattle Kachina is one of the variants of Sikyachantaka.

Holi Kachina

The name of this kachina is taken from the word "Holi" which the kachina constantly sings or shouts. It is said that this version of Holi appeared in Oraibi for the first time in the spring of 1904. He appears in both Kiva and Plaza Dances, usually in the regular dances. The black line across the face is said to represent lightning. This is a good illustration of Holi.

Sio Kachina

The Sio Kachina is the spirit of the Zuni people and is not a Zuni Kachina. He resembles several other kachinas rather closely, notably the Navajo (HSC-137) and the Hornet (HSC-68). He usually appears in a regular dance in the plaza. In this illustration he is carrying a wicker plaque that will probably be given out during the dance.

NIMAN CEREMONY

THE NIMAN OR Home-going performance, given shortly after the summer solstice, is the ceremony that closes the Kachina Season. The date of the Niman is set when the sun reaches its northernmost point. Four days later the initial part of the ceremony begins, and sixteen days later the plaza performance is given. The night before the actual performance is filled with ritual activity and it is nearly dawn before the men hurry to the sponsoring kiva to attach spruce to their masks and costumes. Painted and in full regalia they take their masks to the kachina rest, setting them in a row as they practice their opening song. As soon as their last practice is ended they don the masks and begin their procession to the village with the kachina fathers meeting them along the way. Between the first and second dance interval in the morning the kachinas bring gifts to the audience. Otherwise between each set they return to the kachina rest, and there they unmask and relax, again placing their masks in a row facing southeast.

In the late afternoon when the next to last dance position is taken, the kachina fathers and the Kachina Chief pull up the spruce tree shrine in the plaza and take it to the Powamu Kiva for the final rendition of the last song. While in this position all of the people who have been waiting in the Powamu Kiva come out to bless the kachinas. The Kachina Chief, followed by the kachina fathers, goes down the line sprinkling each dancer with cornmeal. They are fol-

lowed by the Powamu Chief who sprinkles them with medicine water, and the Tobacco Chief who blows a puff of smoke at each kachina. The Tobacco Chief is followed by the Mother of the Kachina Clan and the Mother of the Badger Clan. When they have finished their blessings, they reenter the kiva while the kachinas continue their song. As the kachinas complete their last song, the same people return and each gives the kachinas a prayer feather (a paho) or meal until every kachina has at least one each of the offerings. The kachinas are then dismissed with a formal speech telling them to inform their relatives not to wait but to bring the rain immediately for the benefit of the crops. At the end of the speech the kachinas leave the village. On the following day early in the morning four pairs of kachinas and Eototo and a female impersonator of Kachin Mana appear at the Powamu Kiva, and a rather long and involved ritual is held which, upon completion, closes the Kachina Season until the end of the coming November.

While the Hemis Kachina is the most frequently given impersonation during the Niman Ceremony, he is neither limited to that ceremony nor is he essential to it. Many other kachinas may be used as the Niman Ceremony Kachina, including Kuwan Heheya, Angak' china, Ma'alo, Tasap or even the Sio Hemis Kachina. The Hemis Kachina is most frequently selected because he is a beautiful impersonation, and his songs are popular.

Nuvak´chin Mana

Occasionally among the Kachin Manas of the
Niman Ceremony there will be seen one who has an entirely
white head and face. Snow-white hair will be done up
in a small knot at either side of the head. Above the painted
black eyes is a cluster of small black dots, and on either
cheek the warrior marks appear in black. This kachina
is the Snow Maiden whose function is the same as the
Kachin Mana in the Niman Ceremony. However, she is an
additional prayer for the coming cold weather — the hope
that snow may fall and fill the ground with moisture
for the coming year. In this illustration she kneels,
ready to begin playing the gourd rasp, as she
would during one part of the Niman.

Hemis Kachina

Probably one of the most beautiful and best known
of all Hopi Kachinas is the Hemis Kachina. Often he is
incorrectly called the Niman Kachina from the ceremony
in which he is most often seen. At sunrise, when the
kachinas come to the plaza to dance for the first time, they
bring with them entire corn plants, the first corn harvest
of the year, to distribute to the audience. Against the
backdrop of these magnificant kachinas and their Manas
can be seen a flurry of youngsters carrying the whole corn
plants and brightly-colored presents to the sidelines.
In the Niman or the Home Dance no other kachinas appear,
neither clowns nor side dancers, only the Hemis Kachinas
and their Manas in a double line rotating slowly in opposite
directions, and turning yet again. This final dance of the
kachinas is both stately and reverent. The Hemis Kachina
is presumed to have come from Jemez, a Rio Grande Pueblo.
However, at Jemez Pueblo they have a ceremony in which
the Hemis Kachina appears, and they refer to it
as a Hopi Dance.

214

Hemis Mana

This kachina is the most common female impersonation. Depending upon whom she accompanies or the objects that she holds in her hands, she may be Ahöla Mana, or Qöqöle Mana, Hemis Mana or other Manas. In her appearance with the Hemis Kachina, she plays the rasp during one portion of the performance. This particular instrument is a gourd shell with a padded rim that is turned down to rest on the ground. A notched stick is placed on the gourd and held with the left hand. The right hand holds a sheep scapula so that the central ridge engages the notched stick and then scrapes it up and down. The resulting sound is a coarse grunting tone. Kachin Mana is shown as she emerges from the kiva carrying a resonator.

Sio Hemis Kachina

While the Sio Hemis Kachina is another
introduction from the Zuni in the 1890's, he does not
appear with the Zuni group of Pautiwa, Hakto, and others.
The Sio Hemis may be performed in place of the
more usual Hemis during the Niman Ceremony of mid-July.
In fact, there is little difference between the two except
for the tableta decoration. The tableta of the Hopi Hemis
has towering clouds and rain depicted on it, while that
of the Sio Hemis has dragonflies and sunflowers with
smaller clouds above. Although he appears in the
Niman Ceremony, he may also be seen at other times in the
company of his uncle and the little Spotted Corn Kachinas.
The Sio Hemis is shown here as he would appear when
giving a gift to some small girl or a favorite aunt
in the audience.

216

Hoho Mana

This Zuni maiden usually accompanies the Sio Hemis Kachina, but she may appear with the Hopi Hemis Kachina at Niman. Formerly much more popular than she is today, she was probably introduced among the Hopis some time just before the turn of the century. Hoho Mana has feathers through her ears and wears the woman's high white boots. The ruff about her neck should be crow feathers, and this may be what the artist intended.

ASSOCIATED KACHINAS

MOST OF THE DANCES that are given in the plaza in late spring are accompanied by additional kachinas who may not be dancers. Few dances are given that do not feature clowns appearing both with the dancers and particularly during the kachinas rest periods. Often another group of kachinas will appear either separately or with the clowns; these are the Wawarus Kachinas or runners. The Wawarus Kachinas are a class of kachinas who appear and run races with the men and boys of the village. They come in the late spring, either as a group or as individuals, during the pause in a Mixed or Plaza Dance. Usually they will select one end of the Plaza and, assembling there, will endeavor to have an individual race them. If there are many Wawarus, there will be a great churning about with one or another racing down the length of the Plaza and others prancing up and down to ready themselves for the coming contest.

Quite often they will lure some unwary clown into racing and will immediately catch the hapless individual and perpetrate their peculiar form of punishment on him. They quickly tire of this and will gesture or hold up a reward to some young man in the crowd of bystanders. If he accepts, they will allow him about ten feet of space in which he can move about as he pleases. But the minute he leaves that area he runs as if instant disaster were behind him, and it usually is, for some of the punishments are quite unpleasant. Win or lose he will receive payment with some kind of food from these racers. No one is safe from the oldest man to the youngest boy; all, including white members of the audience can receive the attention of these kachinas. The kachinas are expected to pay for whipping the young men, and this they do by sending water when it is needed for the germinating crops.

In general the kachina runners are stripped to minimum clothing and few encumbrances to hamper their running. Often the eyes and mouth are somewhat larger than those of the usual kachina to facilitate seeing and breathing. The costumes are seldom elaborate and can be improvised from odds and ends. Nevertheless, the type of kachina is easily recognized and his peculiar punishment expected.

Aya Kachina

The name of this kachina is derived from the mask which resembles the rattle given to the children on the occasion of the Powamu or Niman ceremonies. The sun motif appears on both sides of the mask and the rattle. These kachinas come in pairs but race one at a time. In each hand the racer carries a yucca whip with which the runner is given a lusty swat if he does not win the race. The kachina gives piki bread as a reward. The kachina is bearing down on the hapless runner in this illustration and will very shortly deliver a stinging blow with the handful of yucca leaves that he carries.

Wik'china

These kachinas serve the double duty among the
Hopis of being both runners and policemen. As runners,
they rub themselves with grease (Wihu is grease,
hence Greasy Kachina) and soot. When they catch a racer,
they rub grease all over his face and clothes. But they
never whip the unfortunate loser. The illustration shows
the kachina with hands filled with grease and ready
to challenge any runner. The costume of the kachina is
usually not quite so fancy, but this may change with
time and village.

220

Novantsi-tsiloaqa

A translation of the name of this kachina is "He strips you." After catching a racer who does not move rapidly enough, he lives up to his name by ripping the clothing that he can get his hands on. Thus if a person loses to this kachina, he will also literally lose his shirt. The large rayed eyes and mouth and the divided body are the marks of this kachina, though his color may vary. The hair is similar to that of an Iroquois roach. Normally the kachina would not wear jewelry such as the gato on the left wrist because of possible damage or loss.

Hemsona

The name of this kachina comes from the Hopi words for a man's hair knot or queue (nasompi) and hungry; he is the "hair hungry" kachina. He races with a pair of sheep shears, scissors, or knife in one hand. Upon overtaking a challenger, he will fling him to the ground and cut off his hair knot or snip off only a token lock as he sees fit. This kachina is one of the few runners who appears consistently in elaborate clothing on all three mesas. The artist has pictured the kachina flinging a hapless Tcuku or clown to the ground and is preparing to cut off a large piece of his hair.

Puchkofmoktaka

This kachina is called Puchkofmoktaka or Throwing Stick Man on some mesas. At other times he will be known as Scorpion Kachina because the Scorpion carries his own throwing stick on the tip of his tail. Whatever his name, he usually carries two rabbit sticks which are made of cloth and stuffed with cotton. In racing he may either throw these at the individual who escapes him or belabor the unfortunate loser with the dummy sticks. He is sometimes referred to as a hunting kachina. The artist has drawn this kachina as he is seen on the mesas belaboring some unfortunate challenger.

Chöqapölö

This runner is known as the Mud Kachina or the
Clay Ball Kachina. If he catches his victim, he will rub mud
all over his face and hair and into his mouth. The kachina's
costume is really simple as it consists only of mud
smeared all over the body, a breechclout, and a mask.
Although the artist has portrayed this kachina
moving away from the viewer, there is no detail lacking.
The face has only a round black dot for eyes and mouth
and a small red ear on either side of the very simple mask.

Kopon Kachina

This racer is named for the Globe Mallow
that grows at the base of the mesas. He carries a yucca whip,
and those who lose to him will receive a good lashing.
In this illustration the Kopon Kachina has come up to
a Koshari or Hano Clown and is stamping up and down
and offering piki bread to reward the clown for running.
Even though the clown is unhappy at the prospect,
he will still run against the kachina.

Sikyataiyo

The Yellow Fox Runner is often called Sikyataiyo
rather than Sikyataka as shown in Colton. However the
function is exactly the same. Only the name is different.
This racer carries a yucca leaf whip to use on the losers of
a race. The artist has shown him with only a black kilt
or possibly a breechclout, but usually he wears a blue belt
with a long fringe of red hair as well.

Kona Kachina

Kona or the Chipmunk Kachina is distinguishable by his striped forehead. He carries a yucca leaf whip and gives prizes of yellow and red piki bread. Formerly this kachina was extremely plain with a white front separated by a thin black line from the yellow of the remainder of the body. In this illustration the forearms and legs have been painted in the manner usually found on fierce animal kachinas and generally are not on this runner. The face may have either painted rectangular or realistic eyes at the whim of the individual.

Palavikuna

This kachina is known as the Red Skirt Runner or Palavikuna. He carries yucca whips, as do many of the runners, and offers piki bread as a reward for the contestant. The artist has incorporated several variations in his portrayal of this kachina. Normally the ears are made of crossed pieces of wood with red hair attached, and the entire frame is painted the same color. The ruff is usually a foxskin rather than the black and white ruff that is shown.

228

Sivuftotovi

Sivuftotovi or the Dragonfly Kachina
carries a yucca leaf whip and a container of corn smut
that he smears on his victims. If he overtakes his challenger,
he may decide to use the yucca whip rather than smear
his victim. There is quite a range of variation in the
appearance of this kachina. Generally runners do not wear
foxskins or bells around the legs as this interferes
with their speed.

Susöpa

The Cricket Kachina (Susöpa) appears as a racer, although many Hopis will say that he appears only at night in the kivas. This seems to be a difference among villages. Usually this kachina appears with a black bandolier and a tuft of small feathers in place of ears. The kilt he wears is almost universally the folded, plaid, man's shoulder blanket. The hands are painted white. The artist has portrayed this kachina in the act of offering a challenger piki bread. From the disgruntled look on the face of the person accepting the bread, he has just lost the race.

230

Kokopell Mana

One of the few female racers, this mana portrays the erotic female counterpart of Kokopelli, the Humpbacked Flute Player. She will induce someone to run against "her" and then hoist her skirts and overtake him. She flings him to the ground and imitates copulation with him to the unbridled amusement of the audience and the complete discomfiture of the loser. Kokopell Mana stands here in a beckoning pose, attempting to bring forth a challenger.

Kisa

The Prairie Falcon Kachina (Kisa) appears on various occasions though primarily with the Soyohim, and in different costumes. As a runner the small wings on his arms do not usually appear. He carries a yucca whip as punishment for the losers of the race. Most often this racer has a black-tipped bill and pothook eyes. The crest of the head has a small clump of feathers and there is either a wing or an eagle feather at either side in place of the ears to complete the bird impersonation. The warrior marks on the face extend from a brow ring of colored clouds to the ruff. An embroidered kilt is used as a breechclout and is tied with a woman's belt that hangs equally on both sides.

232

Tsil Kachina

Tsil is the Chili Pepper Kachina and a racer. Pursuing his challengers, he will fill their mouths with red pepper powder or an entire pepper if he catches them. In addition to the pepper that he carries in his hand, he has a cluster attached to the top of his helmet. Many times he carries a yucca whip as well. Most times this Racing Kachina is portrayed as being all yellow rather than with the white body that he is pictured with here but it is not an important difference.

Kwitanonoa

Kwitanonoa or the Dung-feeding Kachina is a racer who is particularly unpleasant. The unhappy loser in a race with this kachina may find his mouth stuffed with a ball of dry dung or dregs from the plaza, or have his face smeared with it. Quite often this kachina will carry a yucca whip as the alternate to his other punishment. This is a single kachina with an appearance that differs among the mesas. Colton's number 183 is the Second Mesa variety, and number 247 is the type that appears on First and Third Mesas. This is the Second Mesa form. Kwitanonoa here bends over the hapless clown at his feet, but in this case he does not carry the usual punishment; instead he carries only yucca whips.

Sakwats Mana

Sakwats Mana or the Worm-removing Girl is another of the racing girls. Generally she accompanies the runners on Second Mesa, standing to one side with either a yucca leaf whip or a hair brush in each hand. The racing manas customarily wear a miniskirt so they can move faster than with a regular length woman's dress. The white-faced version is depicted, but she can appear with a blue face and a triangular mouth, women's white boots, or a maiden shawl.

Patung

Patung, or squash, is a favorite kachina for many
collectors. He appears primarily on First Mesa as a runner
and may have been derived from Zuni. Ordinarily
this kachina carries the flower in his right hand and a yucca
whip in his left hand.

THE CLOWNS PLAY an extremely complex role in the Kachina Cult, and it far beyond the scope of this publication to detail their activities in depth. They accompany most Plaza Dances and appear in many of the major ceremonies. If a dancer does not have the proper mask, is late to a dance, or joins a performance at the last moment, he may don a Koyemsi mask and still be included. They are comic relief for some of the dances. Many of the clowns are an object lesson in improper Hopi behavior, but in addition they may serve to cure diseases or function as priests in a Kachina Dance. Some Clowns have a fairly elaborate ceremonial organization while others may appear at the whim of an individual. No matter what their function they universally appeal to the Hopi audience, and their humor ranges from earthy to sophisticated and is usually related to contemporary events.

Koyemsi

Koyemsi or Mud-head Kachinas are probably the most well-known of all the Hopi kachinas. They appear in almost every Hopi ceremony as clowns, interlocutors, announcers of dances, drummers, and many other roles. They nearly always accompany other kachinas; probably the only time when they do not appear with other personages is during the Night Dances. Koyemsi are usually the ones that play games with the audience to the accompaniment of rollicking tunes. These games are generally guessing games, or simple attempts to balance objects or performances of some common act. They most closely resemble our parlor games and the rewards are prizes of food or clothing. This illustration shows a Koyemsi as he would appear with a puppet dancer in the kiva during the Night Dances.

238

Koyala

Koshari or Koyala is the name of a Rio Grande clown that is often seen on the Hopi Mesas. The Hopis very frequently call this clown the Hano or Tewa clown as the Tewa of that village seem to have introduced this personage to the Hopi Mesas. These clowns are considered to be the fathers of the kachinas. They behave in the usual manner of pueblo clowns, engaging in loud and boisterous conversation, immoderate actions, and gluttony. They are often drummers for other dances. This illustration shows the Koshari bending to set down a stack of red and yellow piki, or to offer it to someone in the audience.

239

Piptuka

The Piptuka are not considered in the same light as kachinas. They seem to be a sub-group of the clowns that are improvised only a night or two before their appearance. Any individual may appear as a Piptuka but their function is very close to that of the clowns. They present any form of humor from caricature to burlesque in whatever shape or costume they deem to be appropriate. This Piptuka is apparently burlesqueing a Hopi farmer.

Piptu Wuhti

The Piptu Wuhti is the female version of the Piptuka (HSC-61). They are grotesque caricatures that may be personated on the spur of the moment or to fit a particular circumstance. They are considered to be separate from kachinas as are the Piptuka. They are usually ribald or obscene but always hilariously funny to the Hopi audience. However, they can assume almost any shape age, or characterization of a woman that is desired by the personator. They are not considered to be kachinas but rather improvisations of the moment.

Tsuku

The name Tsuku is synonymous with clown, and there are many forms of Tsuku. They may appear with yellow bodies and red stripes over the eyes or white with black stripes over the eyes. Their actions are antic even though they very frequently follow a traditional form with their humor. They, like the Paiyakyamu or Koshari, make an ash house, carefully outlining its shape and features with ashes from the fireplaces. They run races with the Wawarus Kachina and are the butt of much humor with the Piptuka. They are severely chastised by the Warrior Kachinas such as the Owl for their misbehavior. The vignette shown here depicts three Tsuku with one carrying his "sister" in the back of his belt to help them keep house. The others are busily eating as gluttony is one of their characteristics.

Kaisale

Kaisale is one of the beautiful clowns, so-called because of the many colors that stripe his body. His actions, however, are those of the Tsuku — the Hopi clown. He engages in any outrageous act that will tickle the fancy of the audience. This illustration is typical of his actions as he cavorts about with a watermelon and one old worn out shoe.

White Cloud Clown

Almost nothing is known about this kachina. It is not even certain that the personation is a kachina. Many Hopis have never seen the figure and do not recognize the illustration when they are shown it. His appearance resembles that of a Piptuka rather than a kachina. Presumably his function would be that of the other clowns.

244

HOPI SALAKO CEREMONY

THE HOPI SALAKO CEREMONY is held infrequently. The last Salako on Third Mesa was held in 1912, and the last known on First Mesa was in the 1920's. Second Mesa held one in 1958 and another in 1972. The performance is most often given with the Niman activities and usually supplants the Hemis Kachina. However the last performance on Third Mesa took place in the kivas of Old Oraibi. Because of the infrequent nature of this performance it is one of the least known of the Hopi ceremonies. The earlier authors speak of it as a rumored event and confuse it with the Sio Salako, and even the indefatigable Parsons did not recognize its separate existence until as late as 1937.

The group is usually composed of the following personations, but I suspect others may appear with these; Salako Taka, Salako Mana, Eototo, Hahai-i Wuhti, Sotuknongu, Tukwinong, and two Tukwinong Manas, as well as Tangik'china. The ceremony is very similar in form to that described by Fewkes and Stephens for the Sio Salako. The group is brought into position by Eototo and Hahai-i Wuhti, and specific locations are marked as circles of cornmeal by Eototo. The Salako pair, Salako Taka and Salako Mana, rest in these circles bowing and dipping until beckoned to another set of circles by Hahai-i Wuhti. They advance one at a time to their new positions. Sotuknongu and the Tukwinong with their ceremonial gourds of water and trays of varicolored cornmeal flank the pair. The basic intent is probably that of bringing the cloud supernaturals to the Hopi mesas and causing them to remain in the general vicinity of the villages and fields of the tribal lands.

Tukwinong

The Cumulus Cloud Kachina or Tukwinong appears only on rare occasions and seems to be different on each mesa. The kachina accompanies the Hopi Salako pair. His purpose is that of messenger to the towering thunderheads of summer. He brings water to the thirsty fields of the Hopis. For this reason his helmet is a representation of clouds with falling rain below, he carries water in each hand, and he walks barefoot upon the earth. His body is painted in imitation of the color that is seen below these immense summer clouds when the rain starts. The figure illustrated is that of First Mesa. However, the three semicircular tablets on the head should not circle the head. Instead they should lie parallel from front to back as ridges. The turkey feathers cross only the front part of the face, and the mask behind is usually painted white with black rectangular eyes. The remainder of the head is covered with pendent spruce or fir.

246

Tukwinong Mana

Cumulus Cloud Girl is the sister of Tukwinong, the Cumulus Cloud Kachina. They appear only during the Hopi Salako. As the Hopi Salako is given so seldom, it is very difficult to discover the exact role of this particular kachina, beyond the fact that she would be an assistant to Tukwinong. The blue-gray color of the body is made from the mud that is scoured from the bottom of the springs. The tray that she carries should be filled with meal in a gentle mound and divided into directional colors separated by black lines. The artist has substituted a Hemis tableta for the usual one. The face is that of the First Mesa Tukwinong Mana as shown in Fewkes' *Hopi Katcinas*.

Salako Taka

The Hopi Salako Taka towers seven or eight feet
in the air, a long, slender, shoulderless figure that bows
and dips as he moves in a most graceful manner. He is
always accompanied by his sister, the Salako Mana,
as well as Hahai-i Wuhti and the Tukwinong Kachinas.
The two Salakos are distinguishable only by a few details.
The male has a pink face, earrings that are pendant
eagle plumes and the turquoise-colored moccasins
of the men. This representation would be enhanced by
keeping the tableta to the usual semi-circular form
and emphasizing the hair rather than the shoulders.

Salako Mana

The Salako Mana is the sister of the Salako Taka and they always appear as a pair. Salako Mana is distinguishable from the Salako Taka by her white face and the square turquoise earrings that most unmarried girls used to wear. She is usually somewhat shorter and wears the high white boots of the women. The wraith-like appearance of these kachinas comes mainly from their shoulderless build, an aspect that the artist did not emphasize.

Tangik'china

Tangik'china is the Cloud Guard Kachina.
It is the function of this kachina to appear during the
Salako performance. Usually four of these appear and dance
back of the Cloud Kachinas and the Cloud Kachin Manas,
gracefully waving the willow branches they carry.
This kachina often appears with a headdress very similar
to the Ahul or Wuwuyomo Kachinas
or as it appears in this version.

250

IN MAY, AT ABOUT the time of the spring bean planting, a ceremony is held that is the final act of the initiation year rites. It is an infrequent occurence with as many as thirty years elapsing between rites. It is one of the few times that the Maswik Kachina and his Mana may be seen. Although Masau'u appears in this ceremony also, he appears as a masked god and not as a kachina. Masau'u makes his appearance by circling the village for four consecutive nights until the Maswik Kachinas dance at his shrine on the fourth night. Masau'u joins the Maswik dance, but then he attends to clan rites as the Maswik Kachinas continue to the kivas. Masau'u rejoins them again shortly after they have arrived at the Chief Kiva, and the Maswik Kachinas enter the kiva and continue their dance.

In the afternoon of the next day the Maswik may again be seen. The impersonators (four of them) appear unmasked and play the flute as the young men and girls of the village go to one of the springs to "pick spinach." This "spinach picking" is a ceremonial exchange wherein the boys give the girls flowers, and the girls give the boys packets of food as they gradually progress back to the village. As they reenter the village, they are met by all of the Maswik Kachinas singing and playing flutes as the young people disperse.

Maswik Kachina

The Maswik Kachina is known as the
Masau'u Fetching Kachina or the Skeleton Fetching Kachina
because he announces Masau'u, the raw and bloody
masked god who formerly owned all the land the Hopis
now have and who gave it to them for their use.
The ceremony that the Maswik Kachina announces may be
a reaffirmation of this ancient pact between Masau'u
and the Hopis. When Masau'u appears while the Maswik
are dancing, he is treated with the utmost respect and even
fear by the Maswik Kachinas as well as the assembled
male audience. This dance during the Soyal serves as
a visual announcement of the later dance. This is followed
in the spring by the Nevenwehe or "spinach picking"
ceremony. Normally this kachina dances barefoot with heel
plates. The body is usually quite dark as it is colored
with dried blood.

252

Maswik Mana

Usually the Maswik Kachina alternates with the Maswik Kachin Mana. The Manas appear with the robe wrapped across the chest like a bandolier rather than a cape, and they dance barefoot as do the Maswik Kachinas. This particular Mana is also known as the Jimson-weed Girl, or Chimon Mana, the symbol of which she wears in her hair on the left side. This particular kachina has not been performed in over sixty years. She is pictured holding a black corn ear that is used in sprinkling the Masau'u who appears with these kachinas.

Masau'u

Masau'u (Skeleton Kachina) is the only kachina
who does not go home at the Niman Ceremony and thus
may dance at any time of the year. The organization of the
dance is very much like that of the Niman with the Masau'u
dancing in one line and the Masau'u Mana in the other.
In addition the Skeleton Kachina may appear during
the Pachavu as a pair, with the Wawash Kachina as a racer,
or after a regular kachina dance in the plaza. As he is
a Death Kachina he does many things by opposites,
for the world of the Dead is the reverse of this world.
Thus he may come down a ladder backward or perform
many other common actions in reverse. In addition the
standard Masau'u dance often has antic episodes during
the performance. Occasionally he may appear as a pair
of Masau'u behaving erratically, singing or growling a bit,
beating on the kiva hatchways with willow switches,
or dancing around the fires at the cooking pits and even
through the fires. The many colored splotches on the mask
are alluded to as clouds even though the actual face is that
of a skull surmounted by Soyal prayer feathers.
Masau'u is shown in this illustration carrying somi-viki
(a Hopi food) in his right hand, and various other types
of food on the tray in his left hand which will be
given out during the dance.

254

Masau'u Mana

This is the Mana who comes with the Masau'u or Skeleton Kachina. She appears at any time of the year, as does Masau'u, and dances with him in a separate line as do the Manas with Hemis Kachinas. At times she also kneels and rasps an accompaniment to the Masau'u songs as shown in the illustration. Her face is covered with mud or grayish-brown earth for she is supposed to bring rain. This is an illustration of a Third Mesa Mana.

Selected Readings

Colton, Harold S. *Hopi Kachina Dolls, with a Key to Their Identification.* Albuquerque: University of New Mexico Press, 1959.

Dockstader, Frederick J. *The Kachina and the White Man.* Bloomfield Hills, Mich.: Cranbrook Institute of Science, Bulletin 35, 1954.

Dorsey, G. A., and Voth, H. R. *The Oraibi Soyal Ceremony.* Chicago: Field Columbian Museum, Anthropological Series, vol. 3, no. 1, 1901.

Fewkes, J. W. *Tusayan Katcinas.* Washington, D.C.: Bureau of American Ethnology, 15th Annual Report, 1897.

_____*Hopi Katcinas.* Washington, D.C.: Bureau of American Ethnology, 21st Annual Report, 1903.

Nequatewa, Edmund. *Truth of a Hopi.* Flagstaff: Northland Press, 1973.

Parsons, E. C. *A Pueblo Indian Journal.* American Anthropological Association, Memoirs, no. 32. Menasha, Wis.: 1925.

_____*Pueblo Indian Religion.* Chicago, 1939.

Stephens, Alexander M. *Hopi Journal.* Edited by E. C. Parsons. 2 vols. Columbia University Contributions to Anthropology, vol. 23. New York: Columbia University Press, 1936.

Titiev, Mischa. *Old Oraibi, A Study of the Hopi Indians of Third Mesa.* Cambridge, Mass.: Papers of the Peabody Museum of American Archaeology and Ethnology, vol. 22, no. 1, Harvard University, 1944.

Tyler, Hamilton A. *Pueblo Gods and Myths.* Norman: University of Oklahoma Press, 1964.

Voth, H. R. *The Oraibi Powamu Ceremony.* Chicago: Field Columbian Museum, Anthropological Series, vol. 3, no. 2, 1901.

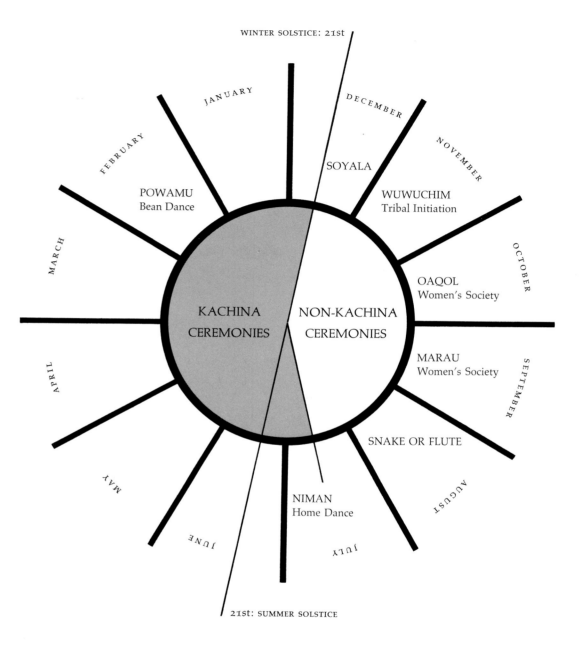

WINTER SOLSTICE: 21st

JANUARY

DECEMBER

FEBRUARY

NOVEMBER

SOYALA

POWAMU
Bean Dance

WUWUCHIM
Tribal Initiation

MARCH

OCTOBER

KACHINA
CEREMONIES

NON-KACHINA
CEREMONIES

OAQOL
Women's Society

APRIL

MARAU
Women's Society

SEPTEMBER

SNAKE OR FLUTE

MAY

NIMAN
Home Dance

AUGUST

JUNE

JULY

21st: SUMMER SOLSTICE

Calendar of major ceremonies

These seven major ceremonies are performed regularly and have certain features in common. Each is conducted by one or more chiefs whose offices are hereditary. Each has eight days of secret rites and ends with a public dance on the ninth day. The primary aim is the production of rain, fertility, and growth.

All ceremonies include the same techniques: offering prayer sticks, building an altar of sacred objects, sprinkling medicine, prayer, song, and dance. The Snake Dance, performed by the Snake and Antelope societies, alternates annually with the Flute Ceremony at the end of August. Although the Snake Dance is widely publicized outside the reservation and is the dance best known to tourists, to the Hopi it is just one of the many rites in their ceremonial calendar.

258

Alphabetical Listing of Kachinas

THIS LIST CONTAINS not only an alphabetical arrangement of kachinas, but also the identification numbers assigned to Hopi Kachinas a generation ago by the late Dr. Harold S. Colton, founder of the Museum of Northern Arizona and a name respected in the study of Hopi Kachinas. This numerical identification system provides a convenient manner for cross reference to many other publications. A few of the kachinas listed were not cataloged by Dr. Colton, and therefore they have no HSC number.

A-ha HSC 10
A-ha Kachin Mana HSC 11
Ahöla HSC 2
Aholi HSC 8
Ahöl Mana HSC 3
A'hote HSC 105
Ahülani HSC 164
Ai Kachina HSC 110
Alo Mana HSC 215
Angak'china HSC 127
Angak'chin Mana HSC 128
Angwushaihai-i HSC 13
Angwusnasomtaka HSC 12
Angwusi, No HSC
Antelope Kachina HSC 90
Avachhoya HSC 122
Awatovi Soyok Taka HSC 26
Awatovi Soyok Wuhti HSC 25
Aya Kachina HSC 48

Buffalo Kachina HSC 93

Chakwaina HSC 160
Chakwaina Sho-adta HSC 162
Chaveyo HSC 37
Chiwap HSC 167
Chöqapölö HSC 53
Choshuhuwa HSC 203

Chospos-yaka-hentaka HSC 140
Chowilawu HSC 20
Corn Dancer HSC 238
Cow Kachina HSC 94

Deer Kachina HSC 91

Eototo HSC 7
Ewiro HSC 202

Flute HSC 106
Fox Kachina HSC 261

Hahai-i Wuhti HSC 44
Hakto HSC 153
Hano Mana HSC 191
Hano Mana HSC 264
Hapota HSC 192
Harvester Kachina HSC 240
Hé-é-e HSC 21
Heheya Aumutaka HSC 36
Heheya Kachin Mana HSC 35
Hemis Kachina HSC 132
Hemis Mana HSC 133
Hemsona HSC 51
Heoto, No HSC
Heoto Mana, No HSC
Hilili HSC 185

Hishab Kachina HSC 193
Hochani HSC 113
Hó-e HSC 40
Hoho Mana HSC 156
Holi Kachina HSC 260
Hólolo HSC 103
Homahtoi Kachina HSC 256
Honan Kachina HSC 89
Hon Kachina HSC 87
Ho'óte HSC 104
Horo Mana HSC 101
Hospoa HSC 207
Hototo HSC 186
Hotsko HSC 80
Hú HSC 14
Huhuwa HSC 125
Hututu HSC 175

I'she HSC 265

Kachin Mana HSC 133
Ka'e HSC 226
Kahaila HSC 145
Kaisale HSC 63
Kaletaka HSC 4
Kana-a Kachina HSC 142
Katoch Angak'china HSC 126
Kau-a Kachina HSC 234

Kau-a Kachin Mana HSC 136
Kawai-i Kachina HSC 181
Kawaika'a Kachina HSC 196
Kisa HSC 72
Kokopelli HSC 65
Kokopell Mana HSC 66
Kokosori HSC 9
Kona Kachina HSC 56
Konin Kachina HSC 143
Kopon Kachina HSC 54
Koroasta HSC 173
Kowako HSC 82
Koyala HSC 60
Koyemsi HSC 59
Koyona HSC 208
Kuwan Heheya HSC 34
Kuwan Kachina HSC 231
Kuwantotim HSC 244
Kwahu HSC 71
Kwasa-itaka HSC 111
Kweo Kachina HSC 86
Kwikwilyaka HSC 107
Kwivi Kachina HSC 169
Kwitanonoa HSC 183
Kyash Kachina HSC 190

Laqan HSC 83

Left-handed Kachina HSC 95
Loi'isa HSC 177

Ma'alo Kachina HSC 130
Mahu HSC 263
Marao Kachina HSC 170
Masau'u HSC 123
Masau'u Mana HSC 124
Mastop HSC 6
Maswik Kachina HSC 115
Maswik Mana HSC 116
Momo HSC 67
Möna Kachina HSC 236
Mongwa HSC 78
Mongwa Wuhti HSC 79
Monongya HSC 69
Motsin HSC 254
Movitkuntaka HSC 172
Muzribi HSC 188

Nakiachop HSC 46
Na-ngasohu Kachina HSC 148
Nataska HSC 29
Na-uikuitaka HSC 235
Navan Kachina HSC 171
Navuk'china HSC 109
Navuk'china HSC 149
Nayaiyataka, No HSC
Nihiyo HSC 245
Novantsi-tsiloaqa HSC 50
Nuvak'china HSC 99
Nuvak'chin Mana HSC 100

Ongchoma HSC 18
Ösök'china HSC 43
Owa-ngazrozro HSC 198

Pachavu Hú HSC 16
Pachavuin Mana HSC 23
Palakwayo HSC 73
Palavikuna HSC 57
Palhik Mana HSC 120
Palölökong Kachina HSC 233
Pash Kachina HSC 197
Paski Kachina HSC 227
Patszro HSC 206
Patung HSC 225
Pautiwa HSC 150
Pawik HSC 75
Payik'ala HSC 168
Piokak HSC 174
Piptuka HSC 61
Piptu Wuhti HSC 252
Poli Kachina HSC 119
Poli Sio Hemis Kachina HSC 246
Pöökang Kwivi Kachina HSC 180
Powamu Kachina HSC 38
Powamu So-aum HSC 39
Puchkofmoktaka HSC 52

Qalavi HSC 17
Qöchaf Kachina HSC 19
Qöqöle HSC 5

Sai-astasana HSC 154
Sakwa Hu, No HSC
Sakwap Mana HSC 165
Sakwats Mana HSC 184
Salako Mana HSC 118
Salako Taka HSC 117
Salap Mongwa HSC 81
Samo'a Wutaka HSC 176
Saviki HSC 121

Shulawitsi HSC 151
Sikyachantaka HSC 253
Sikyataiyo HSC 55
Sio Avachhoya HSC 166
Sio Hemis Kachina HSC 210
Sio Hemis Ta-amu HSC 157
Sio Kachina HSC 262
Sio Salako HSC 158
Sio Salako Mana HSC 159
Sipikne HSC 152
Situlili HSC 211
Sivuftotovi HSC 58
Sivu-i-quil Taka HSC 114
Söhönasomtaka HSC 189
Sohu Kachina HSC 147
Sotungtaka, No HSC
Soyal HSC 1
Soyok Mana HSC 27
Soyok Wuhti HSC 24
Susöpa HSC 64

Tahaum Soyoko HSC 30
Takursh Mana HSC 129
Talavai HSC 168
Tanakwewa HSC 42
Tangik'china HSC 266
Tasap Angak'china HSC 251
Tasap Kachina HSC 137
Tasap Kachina HSC 249
Tasap Kachin Mana HSC 138
Tasap Yeibichai HSC 139
Tatangaya HSC 68
Tawa Kachina HSC 146
Tawa Koyung Kachina HSC 250
Tiwenu HSC 229
Tocha HSC 76

Toho HSC 85
Tokoch Kachina HSC 84
Toson Koyemsi HSC 32
Tsil Kachina HSC 182
Tsitoto HSC 45
Tsuku HSC 62
Tühavi HSC 144
Tukwinong HSC 97
Tukwinong Mana HSC 98
Tuma-uyi HSC 141
Tumoala HSC 243
Tunei-nili HSC 134
Tungwup Ta-amu HSC 15
Turposkwa HSC 74
Turtle Kachina HSC 70
Tuskiapaya HSC 258
Tutumsi HSC 112

Umtoinaqa HSC 237
Üshe HSC 204

White Cloud Clown HSC 259
Wiharu HSC 31
Wik'china HSC 49
Wukoqala HSC 201
Wukoqöte HSC 102
Wupá'ala HSC 96
Wupamo HSC 41
Wuyak-kuita HSC 22
Wuwuyomo, No HSC

Yapa HSC 77
Yoche HSC 205
Yo-we HSC 255
Yung'a HSC 220
Yung'a Mana HSC 221

Index of Kachinas